FRESH from POLAND

FRESH from POLAND

NEW VEGETARIAN COOKING FROM THE OLD COUNTRY

MICHAŁ KORKOSZ

THE EXPERIMENT

NEW YORK

FRESH FROM POLAND: *New Vegetarian Cooking from the Old Country*
Text and photographs copyright © 2020 by Michał Korkosz

The Experiment, LLC
220 East 23rd Street, Suite 600
New York, NY 10010-4658
theexperimentpublishing.com

THE EXPERIMENT and its colophon are registered trademarks of The Experiment, LLC. Many of the designations used by manufacturers and sellers to distinguish their products are claimed as trademarks. Where those designations appear in this book and The Experiment was aware of a trademark claim, the designations have been capitalized.

The Experiment's books are available at special discounts when purchased in bulk for premiums and sales promotions as well as for fund-raising or educational use. For details, contact us at info@theexperimentpublishing.com.

Library of Congress Cataloging-in-Publication Data

Names: Korkosz, Michał, author.
Title: Fresh from Poland : new vegetarian cooking from the old country /
    Michał Korkosz, Saveur award winner.
Description: New York : The Experiment, 2020. | Includes index.
Identifiers: LCCN 2019054739 (print) | LCCN 2019054740 (ebook) | ISBN
    9781615196555 (paperback) | ISBN 9781615196562 (ebook)
Subjects: LCSH: Cooking, Polish. | Vegetarian cooking. | LCGFT: Cookbooks.
Classification: LCC TX723.5.P6 K67 2020 (print) | LCC TX723.5.P6 (ebook)
    | DDC 641.59438--dc23
LC record available at https://lccn.loc.gov/2019054739
LC ebook record available at https://lccn.loc.gov/2019054740

ISBN 978-1-61519-655-5
Ebook ISBN 978-1-61519-656-2

Cover and text design by Beth Bugler
Author photographs by Katarzyna Pruszkiewicz

Manufactured in China

First printing March 2020
10 9 8 7 6 5 4 3 2 1

To the most important women in my life,
my mother and grandmother, who taught me
the greatest joy of cooking

CONTENTS

INTRODUCTION

This story begins with my childish greed. Growing up, I was a fat child who ate everything in sight. Every summer, I would stay with my brother at my grandmother Zosia's house. She, the truest example of a Polish grandmother, derived joy from feeding me constantly. In the morning, when we were still sleeping sweetly under thick eiderdown, she would go to the bakery for fresh buns and bread, and then to the farmers market for the sweetest tomatoes and farm eggs, which she would cook for breakfast with generous amounts of butter, chopped vegetables, and chives. When I woke up, I would spin around her dress, curiously looking at the kitchen stove. She would serve the scrambled eggs in one pan for my brother and me, dividing it in half with a wooden spoon. We would eat, and she would smile at the joy her food would bring us.

My mother also played a fundamental role in shaping my personality and my love of food. Though she's not known for her cooking (she's not a bad cook, though—she makes a few spectacular recipes!), she is the truest gourmand and lover of good food that I know. As I grew up, she would watch mouth-watering culinary programs with me, and then lend me her books, which I read endlessly, choosing the recipes I wanted to try. Then she let

me—at nine years old—try out these recipes, inevitably making a mess in the kitchen as my love of cooking developed. After every recipe I made, I would anxiously await her opinion, hoping she would find my dishes tasty. Most of the time, she liked them! The feeling of joy I experienced when she liked my food was exactly like that which I had seen before in my grandma's eyes.

This is how my passion for food—my inner need to feed myself and others—was born. I discovered that food can not only satisfy the body but also, above all, soothe the soul. This is why I started my blog Rozkoszny, a Polish word that means "delightful." I felt the need to give an outlet to my ideas and make other people happy through my food. *Rozkoszny* refers to those magical moments of the human experience and the most pleasing sensations in the world—which, in this case, are the sensations of making food. The blog creates an environment where readers should first feel fuzzy inside, then suddenly develop an overwhelming appetite. My hope is that my recipes inspire people to run into the kitchen and re-create the delectable dishes to make their day more rozkoszny.

MY POLISH KITCHEN

I was born in Poland and raised on the Polish cuisine of my mother and grandmother. As I learned to cook, I discovered other cuisines—Italian pasta, French desserts, and completely new-to-me Asian flavors. They are exciting, delicious, revealing, but over the years I have discovered that they do not have the one thing I sometimes miss: the nostalgia that can transport me back to the most wonderful, carefree moments of my life. Certain flavors and smells define comfort for me and bring me back to my childhood. Memory, for me, is the sixth taste, and recipes are a crucial part of our heritage.

This book is a self-indulgent journey that reveals my culinary DNA. This is my personal story about Polish cuisine, so don't expect to see only Polish classics. I like to maximize my cooking, which means that I experiment with all my dishes until I cannot improve them any more. I do not avoid butter, honey, gluten, or techniques that enhance taste and sensation. Sometimes, these are very small things that radically change the tone of the dishes, for the better, of course. For example, the lemon zest in the *Leniwe* ("Lazy" Cheese Curd Dumplings, page 26) adds the stunning freshness that is so needed in these pleasant white cheese dumplings.

Remember to treat my recipes as inspiration—cook following your own instincts. If you don't like parsley, which appears frequently, use another herb in its place. Maybe you prefer cilantro, so use that instead! If you can't find cold-pressed rapeseed oil, do not hesitate to substitute extra virgin olive oil in its place. I want to encourage you to adapt my recipes to your individual tastes, as cooking is best when done instinctively.

It may seem strange to you that this Polish cuisine cookbook does not contain meat. For many, Poland is associated with pork schnitzel (known as *schabowy*) and kielbasa sausage, often served with cold vodka. It's true that in the canon of Polish cuisine there are truly stunning meat-based dishes, but here I would like to show my homeland from a different angle. Our valleys are rich in wonderful vegetables and fruits, the culture of dairy products and fermented foods is incredibly advanced, and the number of grain-based dishes is countless. This vegetarian Polish cuisine includes our beloved national comfort food, pierogi, which are made with flour and the Polish farmer cheese *Twaróg* (Polish Farmer Cheese, page 44). In this book, I devote a whole chapter to Polish soups, which taste unlike soups from anywhere else. Each season has its own: in the summer everyone eats chilled pink *Chłodnik litewski* (Chilled Beet Soup with Cucumbers, Radish, and Dill, page 81) with crunchy vegetables; winter is all about the *Barszcz czysty czerwony* (Clear Fermented Beet Soup, page 78), with fermented beet juice and wild mushrooms. I also include the recipe for an amazing soup, *Wegetariański żurek z borowikami* (Żurek with Dried Porcini, page 93), which is made with a sourdough base. My foreign guests are always shocked at how incredible it tastes.

I entrust to you, dear reader, a collection of recipes that—I hope—will awaken your appetite for Poland. Above all, I hope cooking the Polish delights from this book will bring joy to you and your loved ones.

MY POLISH PANTRY

I am not the keeper of a well-organized kitchen. My ingredients are not stored in fancy jars, and they are certainly not arranged alphabetically, by color, or by size. Packages of dried herbs spill out of my cabinet nearly every time I open it. The fridge is small, so it's always too packed with goods that I couldn't resist picking up during my morning shopping. This chaos aside, I tend to have a few ingredients on hand at all times. Most of them are widely available in well-stocked supermarkets or Polish delis.

I do my green shopping in the neighborhood farmers market nearly every day, according to the seasons. Nowadays, globalization has come to Poland; you can buy most fruits and vegetables at any time of year. But if we're being completely honest, strawberries don't have the same stunning sweetness in months other than June; asparagus is the king of early spring; and winter is filled with thousands of varieties of the very best apples. The hardest time of year is the final weeks of winter, when the first spring vegetables are just around the corner. But when spring finally comes, I enjoy the produce even more. Eating the first strawberries of the year is always a big event. I highly recommended following your terroir, eating what nature brings to your table.

Flour

If you enjoy freshly baked bread as much as I do, you should have a few types of flour in your pantry. I use **all-purpose flour** for most baking, but for better results in yeast-based recipes, try **bread flour.** This has a higher gluten content, which allows more gas to be incorporated and trapped in the dough—a fluffier, bubblier bread.

I like the nutty taste of wholemeal, so I always have **whole wheat flour,** which is perfect for my *Pełnoziarnista chałka z migdałową kruszonką* (Whole Wheat Challah with Almond Streusel, page 55). **Rye** is my second favorite grain, mostly used in bread and in this stunning *Miodowe owoce pod żytnią kruszonką* (Rye Crumble with Honey Fruit, page 22).

Flour seems to last forever, but that's just an illusion. It can be stored up to one month before it starts to lose flavor.

Grains

Kasza, particularly **buckwheat,** is a signature of Polish cooking. These dark brown, nutty groats are roasted, but you can also find unroasted buckwheat (*niepalona*)—milder and more delicate in taste before the roasting process. This is a must-try for every foodie. I also always have **pearl barley,** which is a perfect substitute for Arborio rice in risotto. Last, but not least, beautiful yellow **millet** is a real multitasker. It can be used in salads, like in *Sałatka z kaszy jaglanej, rzodkiewek, szparagów i szpinaku* (Spring Millet Salad, page 147). Or you can use it to stuff vegetables, like tomatoes or cabbage rolls. I also love my *Budyń jaglany* (Creamy Millet Pudding with Blueberries and Lemon-Vanilla Honey, page 35), which is hearty and unbelievably creamy.

Cold-Pressed Rapeseed Oil

Rapeseed oil is the most popular oil in Poland for frying, but I am referring to its extra virgin version, which should almost always be used raw. It has a stunning flavor, with notes of nuts, flowers, or even fresh grass. It is truly life-changing, but if you don't have a bottle, you can use a very good, nutty extra virgin olive oil instead.

Butter

As you will see, I have a very French point of view (which also happens to be very Polish): tons of butter! Butter makes everything better, and nobody can deny it. I use only full-fat European-style butter, always unsalted. And brown butter is one of my biggest food weaknesses—as well as a secret weapon in my *Pierogi Ruskie* (page 157).

For frying, I tend to use **clarified butter,** which has a higher smoke point and a much longer shelf life than fresh

butter. It can be stored in the fridge for months.

Cheese

Poland's national cheese is *twaróg*—also known as farmer cheese. I only use the creamy, full-fat kind, *ze Strzałkowa,* which is sometimes available in Polish supermarkets, but you can make your own *Twaróg* (Polish Farmer Cheese, page 44). It's a tangy, creamy, delicious, versatile, and extremely satisfying food. I use this cheese as a topping, filling, and spread, but it's also a fundamental ingredient in my *Sernik* (Traditional Polish Cheesecake, page 180). You can

easily find regular *twaróg* at Polish delis.

I also love sheep's milk ***bryndza,*** which is regional product of the Podhale region, in southern Poland. If you don't have a good Polish deli nearby, you can use feta cheese as a substitute. Another great regional cheese is ***oscypek*** from Zakopane, at the base of the Tatras Mountains. It's a smoked cheese made of salted sheep's milk and is only produced from late April to early October, when the sheep feed on fresh mountain grass. Before that, any milk they produce is needed for the lambs. I like to grill *oscypek* like I would Halloumi cheese, then serve it with a fresh salad filled with crunchy apples.

Soft goat cheese is light, creamy, and spreadable and pairs beautifully with most things, especially sweet, ripe fruits— pear is my favorite. I like to top my grain dishes with a spoonful of this cheese, so that it melts, adding a wonderfully fresh taste.

Parmesan cheese is not a Polish invention, though it first appeared in Poland in the eighteenth century, eaten only by the rich. Nowadays, many Poles tend to use cheaper substitutes produced in Poland. In supermarkets, you can find great hard cheeses such as ***Dziugas*** or ***Bursztyn.*** But sometimes, I like to use real Italian Parmesan in my recipes instead.

Buttermilk, Kefir, and Sour Cream

Poland is a land flowing with milk and honey . . . literally! There are exceptional dairy products, and you can choose from many local companies. I always have a bottle of **buttermilk,** which is a super-underestimated product. The name even contains "butter," which, as you know, I can never get enough of. My *Ciasto drożdżowe* (Yeast-Buttermilk Cake with Berries and Streusel, page 189) stays super-moist and has enormous depth of flavor; *Krem z młodych ziemniaków i maślanki* (New Potatoes and Buttermilk Soup, page 85) has the refreshing taste of Polish summer; and *Proziaki* (Buttermilk Pan Buns, page 60) is the simple result of flour, soda, and buttermilk.

Kefir is a fermented milk drink that can be blissful during hot summer days. In this book, you can switch out buttermilk for kefir, if you prefer a little more punch.

In my fridge, you can always find *kwaśna śmietana*—**sour cream.** The fat content can vary, but most brands contain anywhere from 10 to 22 percent fat. I use 18 percent, which is also the most popular. Nowadays, many people switch out sour cream for yogurt, but for me, it doesn't have the same taste. Nothing can compare with the tangy creaminess of fresh *śmietana*. I serve my pierogi with a scoop of it, and even put some in my *Owsianka* (Creamy Oatmeal with *Kajmak*, Apple, and Walnuts, page 25) for a whole new level of flavor.

Dried Fruits

Apricots, figs, raisins, and cranberries are a true weapon when only apples and pears are in season. I chop and add dried fruits to my morning oatmeal, making it pleasantly sweet. What's more, I constantly use *suska sechlońska*—**smoked plums**—to achieve more umami in meatless dishes; for example, they fill my *Bigos z wędzonymi śliwkami i soczewicą* (*Bigos* with Smoked Plums and Lentils, page 112), with a punch of sauerkraut. This dish fools everybody, because it's so rich but contains no lard. Black garlic, for me, has a pretty similar taste (but it isn't smoked). If you can't find smoked plums, you can use regular prunes with black garlic instead.

I also always have a jar of **candied orange zest.** There is something deliciously extravagant about exotic citrus laden with sugar; it adds a lovely taste to creamy fillings or a luxurious appearance as a final touch, for example, on top of the *Pączki z konfiturą różaną i cytrynowym lukrem* (*Pączki* with Rose Petal Preserves and Lemon Glaze, page 190).

Rose Water, Rose Petals, and Rose Petal Preserves

I am in love with rose flavor. This floral note is a bit grandma-ish, but I don't care. A bottle of Lebanese **rose water** is always on hand. One splash makes everything so special. I highly recommend buying a bottle; you can get it in Middle Eastern delis or online. **Dried rose petals** add a breathtaking final touch to a dish, which is perhaps not the most important for the flavor but is sure to impress all your guests. **Rose petal preserves**—which used to be made by our grandmothers—can be bought in good delis or online, and are perfect for sweetening black tea. Beaten with mascarpone and spread on short pastry, like in the *Różany mazurek z migdałami* (Rose *Mazurek* with Almonds, page 196), it makes one of my favorite treats.

Honey and Sugar

If my recipes call for sugar, I'm always referring to white granulated sugar. I also use powdered sugar, mostly for glazing or dusting. For brown sugar, I always use Demerara sugar, packed into a cup or measured on a kitchen scale.

I am a huge fan of honey. Lucky for me, in Poland there are countless varieties. When shopping at the farmers market, I tend to choose a different one every time. My favorites are honeys made from buckwheat, blueberry, raspberry, and honeydew, which is not blossom nectar but rather a sugary liquid secreted by aphids.

Fermented Foods

In my fridge, there are always a few jars of fermented food, a perfect snack or side dish to something fatty. *Ogórki kiszone* (Salt-Brined Dill Pickles, page 231)—are a classic, available at the farmers market or Polish delis. Fermenting cucumbers at home is easier than people think—and in fact, many Poles do just that. One-week fermented pickles are called *małosolne* ("a little salty"); they are super-crunchy and filled with fresh flavor, a true delicacy of Polish autumn.

Sauerkraut (*kiszoną kapustą*) is a base of many recipes in this cookbook, and a very important part of Polish cuisine. Make sure to use the best you can afford, or ferment your own (page 232). I also recommend trying my *Kiszone rzodkiewki* (Salt-Brined Fermented Radishes, page 235). They're not as popular as sauerkraut or cucumber pickles, but their flavor is extraordinary. A faster way to prepare them (by cheating) is to use the liquid left over from a jar of salt-brined dill pickles. Fermentation should last only 3 days.

Yeast

I always use instant yeast, which, in my opinion, is easier to use. You don't have to make a starter like you would with fresh yeast, or dissolve it in warm water as with active dry yeast. It keeps for many months, and I'm always sure that it will work properly. Since I bake a lot of buns and breads, I always keep a few packets in my pantry. Each packet contains ¼ ounce (7 g) yeast, which is about 2½ teaspoons.

Herbs and Spices

Fresh, fragrant herbs, roughly torn and scattered over a dish, can make even an average meal into something fabulous. I don't have a garden in my small Warsaw apartment, so instead I grow a few herbs in pots. **Rosemary, basil, mint,** and **marjoram** are usually on my windowsill. Dill and parsley, which are essential for my Polish cooking, are sold by bunches in every market on every corner, and I buy them frequently.

I have one culinary weakness: dried herbs and spices. I like having everything in my pantry, to use at any moment. When you open a spice jar, the smell of the spices should be strong. If the scent seems pale, your food will probably also taste pale. The best way to prevent this is by buying herbs and spices in small quantities, more frequently. My essentials are **bay leaves, allspice, fennel seeds, star anise, cloves, cinnamon, caraway seeds,** and **sweet** and **smoked paprika,** which is the most amazing spice. It gives dishes a super-smoky flavor, replacing a meat-based umami, like in my *Fasolka po bretońsku* (Breton Beans with Dried Tomatoes, page 102).

Vodka

Poles have vodka in their veins. In Poland, the culture of drinking vodka is very strong. Every party has to have a bottle, even family gatherings. Many people claim that vodka is tasteless, odorless, and lacking in character, and it's true that the flavor is very difficult to describe. Most Polish vodkas are made with wheat, rye, or potatoes. I once went to a vodka tasting. The flavors of the different vodkas were completely different, but the most impressive part: the finish. You'll feel a punch: in your stomach for rye-based vodka, throat for potato-based, and mouth for wheat-based. Drinking vodka is certainly a learned experience.

But honestly, I prefer to use it for cooking rather than drinking. Especially when it comes to **bison grass vodka** (*Żubrówka*), which has a nice herbaceous flavor. It pairs perfectly with a buckwheat-*twaróg* filling in the *Gołąbki z ziemniakami i kaszą* (Potato-Buckwheat *Gołąbki* with Tomato-Vodka Sauce, page 106). If you can't find bison grass vodka, try another herbal vodka.

BREAKFAST
Śniadanie

Breakfast is my favorite meal of the day, but this wasn't always the case. In childhood, breakfast and I had a fairly complicated relationship. I can't say that I was a fussy eater (though my parents would disagree!), but daily breakfasts were an anguish. My parents made sure that I wouldn't leave the house hungry, so they woke me up really early, as eating anything took me ages.

However, when weekends came along, with lazy breakfasts, the situation changed dramatically. Nobody was rushing and the food started to taste better. There were various bread rolls and generously buttered rye bread; fresh fruits and vegetables; *twaróg,* and *Jajecznica*—eggs straight from the countryside, soft-boiled or scrambled with brown butter (Brown Butter Scrambled Eggs, page 40). As I got older, I realized that I'm not happy to eat the food of duty or physiological need—but I really love to eat for pleasure. I savor the taste and delight in spending time around a table. Nowadays, I happily celebrate every meal, beginning with breakfast.

In Poland, we sit at the table from the early hours. Unlike the habits of Romanesque countries, where breakfast is often eaten on the go or standing at the bar with a croissant or cornetto, Poles have to have a proper seated meal. There is an old adage that says, "Eat breakfast like a king, share your lunch with a friend, and give dinner to your enemy." Well, I like to follow only the first part!

There isn't one characteristic breakfast dish, although breakfast almost always revolves around a grain. Bread, often rye, eaten as *Kanapki* (Sweet and Savory Open Sandwiches, page 39); or with cold cuts, smoked fish, fermented pickles, or scrambled eggs. Sweet-tooths are satisfied with cooked cereals in milk, like *Owsianka* (Creamy Oatmeal with *Kajmak,* Apple, and Walnuts, page 25), wheat or millet puddings, like *Budyń jaglany* (Creamy Millet Pudding with Blueberries and Lemon-Vanilla Honey, page 35). *Twaróg* is essential; it can be served sweet, with honey, preserves, and fruits, or savory, usually as *Gzik* (White Cheese Spread with Radishes, page 17).

On my breakfast menu, there aren't only Polish classics. *Pasta ze słonecznika, koperku i natki pietruszki* (Sunflower Seed Spread with Dill and Parsley, page 18) or *Miodowe owoce pod żytnią kruszonką* (Rye Crumble with Honey Fruit, page 22) are recipes I developed, but I must say—quite immodestly—that they fit perfectly along the other Polish dishes in this book. I also like to experiment on my friends. I often invite them over for breakfast, which sometimes extends to the late afternoon, when we switch out the coffee for something a little stronger. Poles have boisterous breakfasts in their veins. Every Christmas and Easter we have brunches (we simply call these breakfasts), that can last from morning to night and consist of more supper-like dishes. For example, *Gryczane bliny z kwaśną śmietaną i piklowaną cebulą* (Buckwheat Blini

with Sour Cream and Pickled Onions, page 36), is a breakfast that could also be served at an evening party. I appreciate it, because my sense of what constitutes a meal can be very variable. From the early morning I eat *Racuchy* (Apple Fritters, page 29) or *Leniwe* ("Lazy" Cheese Curd Dumplings, page 26) with fried bread crumbs, which, in many Polish households, are eaten for *podwieczorek,* a sweet meal between dinner (which we typically eat around 3:00 or 4:00 PM) and supper (our light evening meal). You only live once, so it's a pity to enjoy such deliciousness for only one meal.

WHITE CHEESE SPREAD
with Radishes
Gzik

Gzik is a cheese spread that differs dramatically depending on who is making it. The basic recipe is so simple that everyone has their own version. It's popular spread on buttered rye bread, but my grandmother Zosia loved to feed me her traditional variety with freshly boiled potatoes and butter. The base of *gzik* is a Polish farmer cheese called *twaróg*, which is sold in thick disks—or you can make your own (page 44). You can substitute *twaróg* with farmer cheese or dry small-curd cottage cheese, adding less sour cream to prevent the recipe from being too runny.

MAKES	PREP TIME
2 cups (480 ml)	10 minutes

9 ounces (1½ cups/250 g) **Twaróg** (page 44), farmer cheese, or small-curd cottage cheese

2 to 6 tablespoons sour cream

1 bunch radishes, finely chopped, saving 1 or 2 radishes for serving

¼ cup (12 g) chopped chives, plus more for serving

1 tablespoon cold-pressed rapeseed oil, plus more for serving

1 teaspoon mustard seeds, ground (optional)

Salt and freshly ground black pepper

1. Mash the cheese in a bowl using a fork, adding 2 tablespoons sour cream to create a smoother texture resembling ricotta. If the mixture is too thick, continue to add up to 4 additional tablespoons sour cream, until you achieve the desired texture.

2. Mix in the radishes, chives, oil, and mustard seeds, and season with salt and pepper.

3. To serve, transfer the *gzik* to a bowl, top with the reserved radishes, more chives, and a drizzle of rapeseed oil. Enjoy with bread or freshly boiled potatoes and butter.

Note: The possibilities for gzik are endless, so use your imagination! Swap out the radishes for cucumbers, or use both. Tomatoes work great here, too. You can also try this spread with parsley, thyme, or finely chopped rosemary.

SUNFLOWER SEED SPREAD
with Dill and Parsley
Pasta ze słonecznika, koperku i natki pietruszki

Warsaw has been named one of the most vegan cities in the world—almost every restaurant has at least two plant-based dishes on the menu. During a Sunday brunch at the Palace of Culture and Science, a beautiful high-rise filled with bars, theaters, and restaurants, I had a chance to try a vegan sunflower seed spread that intrigued me. I had never tasted a spread so creamy, nutty, and tangy. Naturally, I had to re-create this at home. My addition of cold-pressed rapeseed oil makes this herb-rich spread even more special.

MAKES	PREP TIME	SOAKING TIME
2 cups (480 ml)	10 minutes	8 hours or overnight

1¼ cups (150 g) shelled raw sunflower seeds

Scant ½ cup (100 ml) cold-pressed rapeseed oil

1 tablespoon whole grain mustard

1 tablespoon fresh lemon juice

1 cup (30 g) coarsely chopped fresh parsley (about 1 bunch), plus more for serving

3 tablespoons chopped fresh dill, plus more for serving

Salt and freshly ground black pepper

1. Cover the sunflower seeds with water in a bowl. Let them soak at room temperature overnight, or for at least 8 hours.

2. Drain and rinse the sunflower seeds. Transfer to a food processor. Add the oil, mustard, and lemon juice and blend until it reaches a hummus-like consistency. You might have to scrape the sides of the bowl once or twice during processing.

3. Add the parsley and dill and mix together with a spoon. Season with salt and pepper. If the spread is too thick, add some water or more oil and blend until smooth.

4. To serve, transfer the spread to a bowl and top with more parsley and dill. Drizzle liberally with rapeseed oil. Serve on bread.

   Note: *This dip can be made ahead and stored for up to 2 days in the refrigerator.*

PARSLEY ROOT AND WALNUT SPREAD

Pasta z pietruszki i orzechów włoskich

Parsley root is one of my favorite vegetables. An umami gamechanger, it lends an incredible flavor to the classic Polish *Warzywny bulion* (Vegetable Broth; page 77); Roasted, it's addictively caramelized (try it in any grain salad), and my friend Patrycja taught me that it can even be eaten raw, as a crunchy snack, like a carrot. From my love of parsley, this milky, nutty, herby spread was born. It gets its pleasant creamy consistency from cooking the roots in rosemary-flavored milk until they're soft. It's delightful eaten with freshly baked sourdough bread, on a picnic blanket with friends.

MAKES	PREP TIME	COOK TIME
3 cups	10 minutes	20 minutes

1 pound (450 g) parsley root (or parsnip)

3 cups (720 ml) milk

1 sprig rosemary

¼ teaspoon salt

1 cup (100 g) walnuts, coarsely chopped

1 garlic clove

1 teaspoon rosemary, finely chopped, plus more for serving

3 tablespoons cold-pressed rapeseed oil, plus more for serving

1 teaspoon lemon zest

Salt and freshly ground pepper

1. Place the parsley root, milk, rosemary sprig, and salt in a medium saucepan. Bring to a boil; cook, stirring occasionally, until fork-tender, about 20 minutes. Drain, reserving ¼ cup of milk.

2. Combine the cooked parsley root, walnuts, garlic, chopped rosemary, oil, and lemon zest in a food processor. Pulse until smooth, adding the saved milk to get a creamy consistency.

3. To serve, transfer the spread to a shallow bowl, top with rosemary, and drizzle with more cold-pressed rapeseed oil. Eat with your favorite bread.

Note: This spread can be made ahead and stored in an airtight container for up to 4 days in the refrigerator.

RYE CRUMBLE
with Honey Fruit
Miodowe owoce pod żytnią kruszonką

Crumble is one of those foods that works just as well for dessert, with a big scoop of ice cream, as it does for breakfast, with yogurt. This recipe starts with a hefty crumb mixture, studded with nutty rye flour and old-fashioned rolled oats. A bit of butter and sugar ensure the crumb stays crisp after baking, creating a delightful textural contrast between the crunchy topping and tender fruit. Using a mix of sweet stone fruit and tart berries that mix with the natural honey aroma keeps every mouthful of this recipe exciting.

MAKES	PREP TIME	CHILLING TIME	COOK TIME
3 or 4 servings	10 minutes	10 to 30 minutes	40 minutes

FOR THE CRUMBLE

¾ cup (100 g) rye flour

¼ cup (40 g) old-fashioned rolled oats

¼ cup (50 g) Demerara or brown sugar

Pinch of kosher salt

¼ cup plus 1 tablespoon (75 g) unsalted butter, cut into pieces and chilled

FOR THE FILLING

18 ounces (about 2 cups/ 510 g) sliced stone fruit and berries (see Notes)

¼ cup (60 g) honey

1 tablespoon cornstarch

Sour cream or plain full-fat yogurt (optional)

1. **To make the crumble,** toss the flour, oats, brown sugar, and salt in a medium bowl. Add the butter, then use your fingers to rub it into the flour to make a light bread-crumb texture. Chill the crumble for at least 30 minutes in the fridge or 10 minutes in the freezer.

2. Preheat the oven to 350°F (180°C).

3. **To make the filling,** toss the fruit with the honey and cornstarch. Transfer the fruit mixture to a 1-quart (1 L) baking dish.

4. Scatter the crumble over the fruit, then place the baking dish on a baking sheet (to catch any spillover from the fruit juices). Bake until the fruit juices are bubbling and the topping is golden brown, about 40 minutes.

5. Serve warm or cooled with sour cream or full-fat yogurt, if desired.

   Notes: The crumble can be assembled 2 days before baking. Just wrap it in plastic or cover with foil and store in the fridge.

   My favorite fruit combination is raspberries, blueberries, and peaches. Sweet, tart, and juicy, they remind me of my favorite pies. In the fall, I use whatever I can get from the farmers market: mostly apples and pears. But if you don't have access to good fresh berries, frozen ones will work here, too—just bake the crumble a little bit longer.

CREAMY OATMEAL
with *Kajmak,* Apple, and Walnuts
Owsianka

Oatmeal has a bad reputation. People remember it as a soggy nightmare from their childhood. But this hearty breakfast grain can become a delightful meal when paired with the right add-ins. Extremely creamy, with a delicate punch of sour cream balanced with honey, this variation takes oatmeal to a whole new level. Salt is another crucial ingredient—it may seem unnecessary, but it adds depth to the oatmeal and balances the other flavors. I like to top mine with juicy apple chunks, crunchy walnuts, and a tablespoon of good *kajmak* (Polish dulce de leche). Life's too short—so why not let breakfast be more like dessert?

MAKES	COOK TIME
2 servings	15 minutes

⅔ cup (80 g) old-fashioned rolled oats

Big pinch of salt

¼ cup (60 g) sour cream

2 tablespoons honey

2 tablespoons *kajmak* (see Note) or dulce de leche

1 medium Granny Smith apple (7 ounces/200 g), cored and chopped

2 tablespoons (20 g) chopped walnuts

1. Combine the oats, 1½ cups (360 ml) water, and the salt in a medium saucepan. Cook over low heat, undisturbed and uncovered, until oats absorb all the liquid, for 7 to 8 minutes. (Do not stir.)

2. Add the sour cream, honey, and another ¼ cup (60 ml) water to the oats. Stir to combine. Simmer uncovered, stirring occasionally, for 2 to 3 minutes, until thickened.

3. To serve, divide oatmeal between bowls. Top each with 1 tablespoon *kajmak,* half of the chopped apple, and 1 tablespoon walnuts.

Note: To make homemade kajmak, *place a 14-ounce (400 g) can sweetened condensed milk in a large saucepan and cover it with water by 1 to 2 inches. Bring it to a very gentle boil, then reduce the heat to low and cook for 3 hours. Do not let the water drop below the top of the can during cooking. Let cool completely before opening the can. Store in the fridge for up to 1 month.*

"LAZY" CHEESE CURD DUMPLINGS
Leniwe

Leniwe means "lazy," which is the perfect word for these dumplings. Traditionally served in Poland as a comforting late-breakfast treat or even as a sweet lunch, they have a delightful texture that melts in your mouth and a complex, slightly sour flavor. *Leniwe* are usually made with curd *twaróg,* but if you prefer creamier ones (like I do), use a smoother cheese, or blend the cheese first. The secrets to my dumplings are the lemon zest, which makes them fresh and vibrant, and my technique: I make the "lazy" dumplings very lazily and they turn out perfect every time.

MAKES	PREP TIME	COOK TIME
2 to 4 servings	10 minutes	10 minutes

FOR THE DOUGH

9 ounces (1½ cups/ 250 g) *Twaróg* (page 44) or smooth farmer cheese

1 large egg

1 teaspoon grated lemon zest

1 tablespoon sugar

⅓ cup (40 g) all-purpose flour, plus more as needed

FOR THE TOPPING

3 tablespoons fresh or dried bread crumbs (see Note)

1 teaspoon sugar

Pinch of salt

2 tablespoons (30 g) unsalted butter

1. To make the dough, mash together the cheese, egg, lemon zest, and sugar with a fork in a medium bowl. Add the flour and stir to combine.

2. Transfer the dough to a floured board. Keep folding until the dough is smooth and elastic, adding more flour if needed.

3. Divide the dough into two balls. Roll each ball into a long, thin rope about 12 inches (30 cm) long. Slice the ropes on the diagonal into 1-inch (2.5 cm) pieces.

4. Bring a large pot of water to a boil. Drop in the dumplings, in batches if necessary. When they float to the surface after 2 to 3 minutes, remove them with a slotted spoon, transfer to a colander, and drain.

5. To make the topping, heat a medium skillet and toast the bread crumbs until they start to turn golden brown, 1 to 2 minutes. Add the sugar, salt, and butter. Fry, stirring frequently, until the bread crumbs and butter are combined.

6. To serve, divide the dumplings among plates. Top with the buttered bread crumbs.

Note: I usually use store-bought bread crumbs, which are finely ground. You can also use a white rustic bread without crust for a homemade variety: Cut the bread into 1-inch (2.5 cm) pieces and pulse in a food processor until crumbs form.

APPLE FRITTERS
Racuchy

Because *racuchy* are so versatile, I had trouble deciding where this recipe should go in the book. I eat them for a sweet lunch, a light dinner, or a late breakfast—and so does everyone else I know! Sometimes, I make them with a yeast dough, but it's much more time consuming. This version is just as delicious and so much easier.

MAKES	PREP TIME	COOK TIME
2 or 3 servings	5 minutes	15 minutes

1 cup (130 g) all-purpose flour

1 tablespoon granulated sugar

¾ teaspoon baking soda

¼ teaspoon salt

¾ teaspoon ground cinnamon

1 large egg, lightly beaten

¾ cup (180 g) buttermilk

2 medium Golden Delicious apples, peeled, cored, thinly sliced, and chopped (about 3 cups/400 g)

2 tablespoons (30 g) clarified butter

Powdered sugar

Brown Butter Applesauce with Cider (page 224)

1. Whisk the flour, sugar, baking soda, salt, and cinnamon in a large bowl. Add the egg and buttermilk; whisk to combine. Fold in the chopped apples.

2. Heat the clarified butter in a large nonstick skillet over medium heat. Allow the butter to cover the entire bottom of the pan. Scoop 2 tablespoons of the batter into the skillet for each fritter, spacing them well apart. Cook until golden brown on one side, 2 to 3 minutes, then flip and cook until browned on the other side, 2 to 3 minutes longer. Remove from the skillet using a slotted spoon and drain briefly on paper towels. Repeat with the remaining batter.

3. To serve, dust with powdered sugar and spread with applesauce.

   Note: You can omit the apples (many Poles do that), or switch them out for another fruit, like chopped plums, or strawberries, blueberries, or raspberries.

PANCAKES
with White Cheese and Rose
Naleśniki

At my house, there were always *naleśniki* (pancakes) waiting for me on Fridays after school. At school, I would dream about what I'd eat when I got home. There were so many options: my mom's strawberry preserves, chocolate spread (my favorite at the time), or white cheese and seasonal fruits. My dad stood over the stove, frying tons of pancakes for me and my friends. Hovering over the hot pan for hours was his simple, wordless way of showing love. I like to think I inherited this from him, because I love to make these pancakes for my loved ones. What I love about these pancakes is that they're thin but soft at the same time, a result of the sparkling water, which makes the batter fluffier. I usually serve them for a weekend breakfast, stuffed with soft *twaróg,* candied orange zest, and rose petals, but they are even better the next day, reheated in butter—which is how I often eat them, after my guests have gone home.

MAKES	PREP TIME	COOK TIME
6 to 8 pancakes	10 minutes	30 minutes

FOR THE PANCAKES

¾ cup (100 g) all-purpose flour

¼ teaspoon salt

½ teaspoon sugar

½ cup (130 ml) milk

½ cup (130 ml) sparkling water

1 large egg

2 tablespoons plus 1 teaspoon (35 g) unsalted butter, melted

1 tablespoon (15 g) unsalted butter

FOR THE FILLING

9 ounces (1½ cups/250 g) *Twaróg* (page 44) or smooth farmer cheese (see Note)

4 ounces (½ cup/110 g) fromage frais or sour cream, plus more for serving

2 egg yolks

¼ cup (50 g) sugar

2 tablespoons finely chopped candied orange zest

1 tablespoon rose water

Pinch of salt

Unsprayed rose petals

recipe continues . . .

1. **To make the pancake batter,** put the flour, salt, sugar, milk, water, egg, and 1 teaspoon of the melted butter in a stand blender and pulse to combine.

2. Heat a medium (9 inch/23 cm) nonstick skillet over medium-high. Lightly brush with 1 tablespoon of the melted butter. Pour 3 to 4 tablespoons batter into the skillet and swirl to coat the bottom evenly. Cook the pancake until bubbles form on the surface and the edges are golden and crisp, 2 to 3 minutes. Loosen the edge of the pancake with a rubber spatula, then carefully and quickly flip. Cook until brown spots appear on the second side, about 1 minute. Set the pancake aside on a plate. Repeat with the remaining batter, brushing the skillet with additional melted butter if needed.

3. **To make the filling,** mash together the cheese and fromage frais in a medium bowl until well combined. Add the egg yolks, sugar, orange zest, rose water, and salt, and stir to combine.

4. Place 1 pancake on a flat surface. Place 2 tablespoons of the filling in the middle and fold the sides up over the center. Starting at the bottom, roll the pancake to enclose the filling. Repeat with the remaining pancakes and filling.

5. Melt 1 tablespoon butter in a cast-iron skillet over low heat. Fry the filled pancakes until golden brown and crispy on both sides, about 2 minutes per side. Garnish with rose petals before serving.

   Note: If you can't find twaróg *or farmer cheese, you can use ricotta, which gives the filling a creamier consistency but less of a tangy flavor.*

CREAMY MILLET PUDDING
with Blueberries and Lemon-Vanilla Honey
Budyń jaglany

It's hard to believe that this incredibly luscious pudding is a breakfast option. Its structure is silky and creamy; it melts in the mouth. Cooking millet with chopped apple gives it a bit of sweetness and makes it even fluffier. You can top your pudding with whatever you desire, but this juicy blueberry sauce and lemon-vanilla honey are the toppings of my dreams.

MAKES	COOK TIME
2 servings	15 minutes

FOR THE MILLET PUDDING

½ cup (100 g) millet

2⅓ cups (560 ml) milk

1 medium apple (7 ounces/ 200 g), peeled, cored, and chopped

Pinch of salt

1 teaspoon honey

1 teaspoon (5 g) unsalted butter

FOR THE BLUEBERRY SAUCE

½ cup (80 g) fresh or frozen blueberries

1 teaspoon fresh lemon juice

1 tablespoon sugar

FOR THE LEMON-VANILLA HONEY

3 tablespoons honey

2 tablespoons fresh lemon juice

1 vanilla bean, split lengthwise

1. **To make the millet pudding,** rinse the millet with hot water and drain it well. Bring 2 cups (480 ml) of the milk to a boil with the apple and salt. Stir in the millet; cook covered on low heat, until all the liquid has been absorbed, about 15 minutes.

2. Transfer the cooked millet and apple to a stand blender. Add the honey, butter, and ¼ cup (60 ml) of the remaining milk; blend until smooth. Stir in the remaining milk to obtain a puddinglike consistency.

3. **To make the blueberry sauce,** put the blueberries, lemon juice, and sugar in a small saucepan. Bring to a boil, then remove from the heat.

4. **To make the lemon-vanilla honey,** combine the honey and the lemon juice in a small bowl. Scrape in the vanilla bean seeds and stir to mix them through. (Save the pod for another use.)

5. To serve, divide millet pudding among bowls. Top with blueberry sauce and lemon-vanilla honey.

BUCKWHEAT BLINI
with Sour Cream and Pickled Red Onions
Gryczane bliny z kwaśną śmietaną i piklowaną cebulą

I don't trust people who claim that blini are old-fashioned. These supple buckwheat pancakes are a sumptuous way to celebrate every day. Topped with capers and pickled red onions for an invigorating touch, these blini are served with an obligatory dollop of sour cream and a bit of fresh dill.

MAKES	PREP TIME	CHILLING TIME	RISING TIME	COOK TIME
about 14 large blini	15 minutes	2 hours	1 to 1½ hours	15 minutes

FOR THE PICKLED ONIONS

2 medium red onions (about 10 ounces/300 g total), very thinly sliced

¼ cup (60 ml) apple cider vinegar

¼ cup (50 g) sugar

4 allspice berries

2 whole cloves

FOR THE BLINI

1 cup (140 g) buckwheat flour

1 cup (130 g) all-purpose flour

One ¼-ounce (7 g) packet instant yeast

½ teaspoon salt

½ teaspoon sugar

1 cup (240 ml) lukewarm milk

2 tablespoons sour cream

3 tablespoons (45 g) unsalted butter, melted, plus more for frying

3 large eggs, yolks and whites separated

FOR SERVING

Sour cream

Capers

Chopped fresh dill

1. **To pickle the onions,** pack the onions into a clean mason jar. Combine the vinegar, sugar, ½ cup (120 ml) water, allspice berries, and cloves in a small saucepan. Bring to a boil; stir to dissolve the sugar. Pour the pickling liquid into the jar, covering the onions completely. Let cool to room temperature, then chill.

2. **To make the blini batter,** while the onions are chilling, mix the buckwheat flour, all-purpose flour, yeast, salt, and sugar in a large bowl. Add the milk, sour cream, butter, and egg yolks. Whisk until smooth. Cover the batter and let sit in a warm place until doubled in volume, 1 to 1½ hours.

3. In a medium bowl, whisk the egg whites until they form soft peaks; fold gently into the batter.

4. Preheat the oven to 200°F (100°C). Line a baking sheet with a wire rack and place it in the oven.

5. Lightly brush a large nonstick skillet with melted butter over medium heat. Pour in 2 tablespoons batter to make each 3-inch (8 cm) blini, spacing them well apart. Cook until bubbles form on top and begin to pop, 2 to 3 minutes. Flip the blini and cook until golden brown on the other side, about 2 minutes. Transfer the blini to the wire rack to keep warm in the oven. Repeat with the remaining batter, brushing the skillet with butter as needed.

6. To serve, arrange the blini on a platter. Spoon about 1 teaspoon sour cream over each one. Top with some pickled onion and capers and garnish with dill.

Notes: You can make the batter ahead through Step 2, cover it, and chill for 8 to 12 hours. Bring to room temperature before cooking.

The pickled onions can be stored in the fridge up to 2 weeks.

SWEET AND SAVORY OPEN SANDWICHES

Kanapki na słono i słodko

A *kanapka,* like a French tartine, is nothing more than a slice of good bread topped with whatever you like. Open sandwiches, often buttered, with slices of ham, cheese, and sweet tomato, are probably the most popular fast breakfast food in Poland. But I like to treat a *kanapka* as a painting, where only my creativity is the limit. Every time I make them, I top my *kanapki* with something different. Here are a few of my favorite combinations.

PREP TIME
about 5 minutes

SWEET

Sour Cream, Strawberries, Honey, and Mint

Spread a slice of toasted challah with butter and sour cream. Top with roughly sliced strawberries and fresh mint. Drizzle with honey.

Butter, Bittersweet Chocolate, and Chile

Spread a slice of challah with a butter. Top with roughly chopped chocolate and chile flakes. Heat in the oven until the chocolate melts and the bread is toasted, 5 minutes at 395°F (200°C).

Twaróg, Cucumber, and Honey

Season thinly sliced cucumber with fresh lemon juice, salt, and pepper. Spread a slice of sourdough bread with *twaróg* and top with the cucumber and a drizzle of honey.

Twaróg, Raspberry Preserves, and Rose Petals

Spread a slice of toasted challah with *twaróg.* Top with raspberry preserves and rose petals.

SAVORY

Oscypek Cheese, Tart Apple, and Marjoram

Grill oscypek cheese or smoked mozzarella in a grill pan or a skillet, until slightly melted. Top a slice of sourdough bread with slices of apple and the cheese. Season with dried marjoram.

Mayonnaise, Tomato, Lime Juice, and Fresh Dill

Spread a slice of toasted sourdough bread with mayonnaise. Top with sliced ripe tomato and chopped dill. Drizzle with fresh lime juice. Season with flaky sea salt and freshly ground black pepper.

Soft Goat Cheese, Pear, Walnuts, and Rosemary

Spread a slice of toasted sourdough bread with soft goat cheese. Top with sliced ripe pear, chopped walnuts, and fresh rosemary. Drizzle with honey.

Butter, Radishes, Cracked Black Pepper, and Sea Salt Flakes

Season room-temperature butter with cracked black pepper. Spread a slice of sourdough bread with the peppery butter and top with thinly sliced radishes. Sprinkle with flaky sea salt.

BROWN BUTTER SCRAMBLED EGGS
Jajecznica

Jajecznica reminds me of Sunday family breakfasts, when everyone is hungry and no one is in a hurry. I will never forget the taste of the *jajecznica* that my grandmother used to make for me and my brother. She would serve it in one skillet for both of us, gently drawing two portions with a wooden spoon. I always ate mine with a roughly chopped tomato and dill or chives, which is how I still eat it today. The only change I've made is that I brown the butter to give the scrambled eggs a nuttier, creamier flavor.

MAKES	PREP AND COOK TIME
2 servings	10 minutes

2 tablespoons (30 g) unsalted butter

4 large eggs

Flaky sea salt and freshly ground black pepper

Chopped fresh chives

Chopped or sliced tomatoes

Sourdough bread

1. Heat the butter in a medium skillet over medium heat until golden brown and fragrant, 3 to 4 minutes. Remove from heat.

2. Whisk the eggs with an immersion blender or a fork; season with salt and pepper. Add the eggs to the skillet with the hot brown butter. Cook over high heat, whisking constantly, until barely set, about 2 minutes.

3. Divide the eggs between two plates and sprinkle with chives and sea salt. Serve with tomatoes and sourdough bread.

BUTTERMILK-HONEY FRENCH TOAST

Tosty francuskie na maślance

French toast wasn't always fancy. My dad called it "eggy bread," because he made it by dipping bread only in egg. Nowadays, on indulgent weekends, I soak stale day-old challah in a buttermilk mixture, which gives it a more complex flavor. With a drizzle of warm, runny honey that sticks to your hands, this French toast is the best reason to wait for Sunday.

MAKES	PREP TIME	COOK TIME
2 servings	5 minutes	15 minutes

2 large eggs

⅔ cup (160 g) buttermilk

⅓ cup (80 ml) milk

1 tablespoon honey, plus more for serving

½ teaspoon pure vanilla extract

Pinch of salt

Six ¾-inch-thick (2 cm) slices challah or brioche, preferably one day old

2 tablespoons (30 g) unsalted butter

2 tablespoons vegetable oil

1. In a large bowl, beat the eggs with the buttermilk, milk, honey, vanilla, and salt until blended. Working with one slice at a time, soak the bread in the egg mixture, turning several times. Set them aside on a plate.

2. Heat 1 tablespoon of the butter and 1 tablespoon of the vegetable oil in a large skillet over medium-low heat. Add half the bread slices to the pan and cook until golden brown on the underside, 3 to 4 minutes. Flip and cook until golden brown on the other side, 2 to 3 minutes longer. Remove from the pan and transfer to a plate lined with a paper towel to cool. Repeat with the remaining bread, adding an additional tablespoon each butter and oil to the skillet.

3. To serve, arrange the French toast on a large platter and drizzle with honey.

   Note: If you want to use the Whole Wheat Challah (page 55), soak the bread in the buttermilk mixture, pressing down gently until it is saturated but not soggy, for about 10 minutes.

POLISH FARMER CHEESE
Twaróg

I have to admit that I wasn't always a big fan of *twaróg*. But everything changed when I tried a creamy version from Strzałkowo, a small town in western Poland; it truly melts in the mouth. When I don't have access to it, I make my own *twaróg*. It's fatty and creamy and perfectly replaces the store-bought variety. A slice of freshly baked, buttery challah with homemade *twaróg* and honey is a real delicacy.

MAKES	PREP TIME	COOK TIME	RESTING TIME	CHILLING TIME
1½ pounds (675 g)	15 minutes	1 hour	1 hour	2 hours

2 quarts (2 L) buttermilk

2 cups (480 ml) heavy cream

2 cups (480 ml) sour cream

¼ teaspoon salt (optional)

1. Combine the buttermilk, heavy cream, and sour cream in a large pot. Cook, uncovered, over low heat, for 50 to 60 minutes, until the cheese curds separate from the liquid whey. Turn off the heat and let it sit, covered, for an hour. (This helps the curds separate as well.)

2. Place a layer of cheesecloth over a large colander set inside a large bowl. Pour the curds into the cheesecloth. The liquid whey will drain and collect in the bowl and the solid curds will remain in the cheesecloth (see Note).

3. Gather up the edges of the cheesecloth and tie a string around the top to form a bundle. Chill and continue to drain in the colander inside the bowl, for at least 2 hours.

4. Place the *twaróg* in a container and mix with the salt, if desired. Store in the fridge for up to 5 days.

   Note: Don't discard the whey. Instead, use it as a protein boost in smoothies or as a refreshing drink on its own. Store it in a sealed container in the refrigerator for up to 1 week.

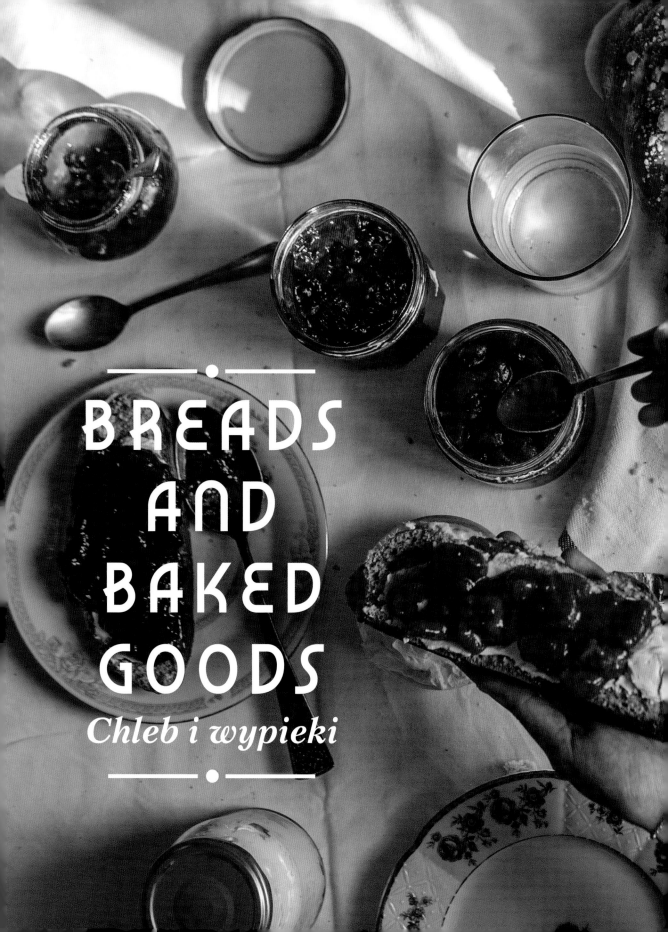

BREADS AND BAKED GOODS

Chleb i wypieki

Freshly baked bread is one of my favorite smells. I love to go to the bakery, even if I don't need to buy anything. I simply walk around, blissfully staring at the big loaves coated with lots of flour. I listen to the sound of the crust, when the ladies behind the counter give customers their favorite bread, and I imagine its crunchiness and flavor. Nothing comforts me like a slice of freshly baked sourdough bread, lavishly buttered. That's the taste of my home.

So when I moved out of my childhood home to study at the University of Warsaw, I missed the bread, or rather the warmth and harmony that is associated with it. In the first few months, I felt emptiness, longing, and loneliness. Of course, in Warsaw, you can buy bread anywhere, but the loaves didn't have the taste that I remembered from home. And at that time, I wasn't able to bake it myself. The kitchen in my new apartment was very small and the oven didn't work properly. Then, after some time, in one of the bakeries at the other end of the city, I discovered the perfect loaf. I went back to this bakery every Monday evening, bringing home a loaf of whole wheat sourdough bread. I would slice it, leaving bread crumbs all over the kitchen counter, and then eat it with lots of butter. I started to feel the familiar tastes of home that I missed so much.

In Polish culture, bread plays a fundamental role. Traditionally, newlyweds are welcomed with bread and salt, symbolizing prosperity and durability. This tradition dates back to the Slavonic times. Under the great Polish dynasties, the Jagiellonian and Piast, the wealth of the country was based on salt mined in Bochnia and Wieliczka. The bread was the basis of life, satisfying the hunger of thousands of people. In religious symbolism, the bread is identified with the body of Jesus Christ, and to this day, a cross is often cut into the top.

ONION–POPPY SEED BUNS
Cebularze

This recipe was inspired by *cebularze lubelskie,* wheat buns topped with diced onion and poppy seeds, from the city of Lublin in southeastern Poland. And, my oh my, are these buns good! They're soft and vaguely sweet, thanks to the caramelized onion–apple topping, but have a crunchiness in every bite—in other words, they are exactly how a savory bun should taste. Don't skip the poppy seeds; they are part of what make these buns so special.

MAKES	PREP TIME	RISING TIME	BAKE TIME
12 buns	20 minutes	1½ hours	20 minutes

FOR THE DOUGH

4 cups (520 g) all-purpose flour

Two ¼-ounce (14 g total) packets instant yeast

1 tablespoon sugar

1 tablespoon salt

¼ cup (60 ml) cold-pressed rapeseed oil or another neutral oil

Scant 1 cup (220 ml) warm milk

1 tablespoon sour cream

FOR THE TOPPING

2 tablespoons (30 g) unsalted butter

5 small white onions (1¾ pounds/800 g total), thinly sliced

1 teaspoon sugar

1 medium tart apple (about 7 ounces/200 g), such as Granny Smith, peeled, cored, and chopped

1 large egg

1 tablespoon milk

2 tablespoons poppy seeds

1 tablespoon flaky sea salt

2 tablespoons cold-pressed rapeseed oil

Salt and freshly ground black pepper

1. For the bun dough, whisk the flour, yeast, sugar, and salt in the bowl of a stand mixer fitted with a paddle attachment to combine. Stir in the oil, milk, and sour cream. Using the dough hook attachment, mix on medium speed until a smooth, soft dough forms, 5 to 6 minutes. Cover with plastic wrap or a kitchen towel and let rise in a warm spot until doubled in size, 1 to 1½ hours.

2. While the dough rises, make the filling. Heat the butter in a large skillet over medium heat. Add the onions, sugar, and a pinch of salt. Cook, stirring occasionally, until the onions begin to brown, about 15 minutes. Add the apple and cook, covered, on low heat until soft, 5 to 10 minutes. Season with more salt and pepper, to taste. Let cool.

3. Gently deflate the dough and divide it into 12 pieces. Shape each piece into a round ball; flatten to about 4 inches (10 cm) across. Place the buns on a parchment paper-lined baking sheet. Place a heaping tablespoon of the topping on top of each one.

4. Beat the egg and milk together in a small bowl. Gently brush the egg wash along the edges of the buns, then sprinkle with the poppy seeds and sea salt. Cover and let rise for 30 to 45 minutes, until noticeably puffy.

5. Preheat the oven to 375°F (190°C). Bake the buns for 20 minutes, or until golden. Remove from the oven, and brush with the rapeseed oil before serving.

   Note: Cebularze taste best while warm. But if you have leftovers and need to reheat them, place the buns on a baking sheet, tent lightly with aluminum foil, and bake for 10 minutes in a preheated 350°F (190°C) oven.

NO-KNEAD MORNING BREAD
Bezproblemowy chleb pszenny

I inherited a huge love of bread from my mom. She's made me so many beautiful loaves of bread, but she always wants everything to be done quickly. So she made this no-knead bread, which is simply mixed with a wooden spoon. Watching her prod at the dough always made me laugh, and now that I make my own, it's shocking how easy it is. This chewy, crunchy, still-warm bread in the morning—just the way Mom makes it—is so delicious.

MAKES	PREP TIME	RISING TIME	COOK TIME
1 loaf	10 minutes	12 hours	50 minutes

3½ cups (450 g) all-purpose flour, plus more for dusting

1 teaspoon (3 g) instant yeast

2 teaspoons salt

1. Stir together the flour, yeast, and salt. Add 1½ cups (350 ml) room-temperature water and stir with a wooden spoon until all the flour is moistened. The dough should be quite shaggy. Cover the bowl with plastic wrap and let rest at room temperature overnight, 8 to 12 hours.

2. About 1 hour before baking, arrange a rack in the middle of the oven. Place a large covered Dutch oven on the rack. Preheat the oven to 475°F (250°C).

3. Lightly flour a work surface and turn the dough out onto it. Sprinkle it with a little more flour and fold the dough over onto itself twice. Quickly shape the dough into a round ball. Cover with a kitchen towel and let sit until the oven has heated, at least 30 minutes.

4. Remove the lid from the Dutch oven and place the dough inside. Slash the top of the dough with kitchen shears or a sharp knife. This will help the bread expand while baking.

5. Return the lid to the Dutch oven and bake for 30 minutes, until the bread is fully risen. Remove the lid and continue to bake for an additional 20 to 30 minutes, or until the top of the bread is a deep golden brown.

6. Using a knife or spatula, carefully remove the bread from the Dutch oven. Cool on a wire rack at least 30 minutes before slicing.

   Note: If you don't eat the whole loaf, store it at room temperature, wrapped in a kitchen towel and a plastic bag. Sliced bread can be frozen for up to 3 months.

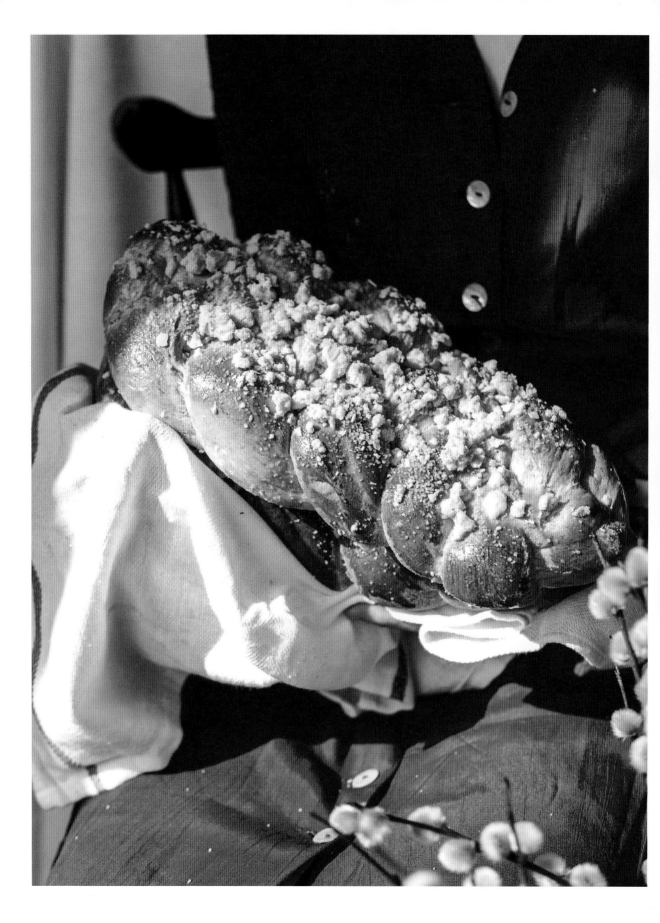

WHOLE WHEAT CHALLAH
with Almond Streusel
Pełnoziarnista chałka z migdałową kruszonką

What's wonderful about challah is that it can be used in so many ways. As a child, I ate a few slices for breakfast every Friday, with butter and preserves, carefully picking out the raisins. (I hate raisins!) On Saturdays, the challah was soaked in eggs and milk, then fried to golden brown and dusted with powdered sugar. On Sundays, we ate it toasted with fabulously melty cheese. Baking challah is very rewarding. Everyone loves this whole wheat version, which has a nuttier flavor. I sprinkle it with buttery almond streusel, which gives it a richer flavor.

MAKES	PREP TIME	RISING TIME	COOK TIME
2 loaves	20 minutes	50 minutes	40 minutes

FOR THE DOUGH

3 cups (420 g) bread flour, plus more for dusting

2 cups (280 g) whole wheat flour, preferably stone-ground

½ cup (100 g) granulated sugar

Two ¼-ounce packets (14 g total) instant yeast

Salt

2 large eggs

2 egg yolks

¼ cup (½ stick/60 g) unsalted butter, melted

FOR THE ALMOND STREUSEL

3 tablespoons whole wheat flour

2 tablespoons almond flour

3 tablespoons Demerara or brown sugar

¼ teaspoon salt

2 tablespoons (30 g) unsalted butter, chilled

recipe continues . . .

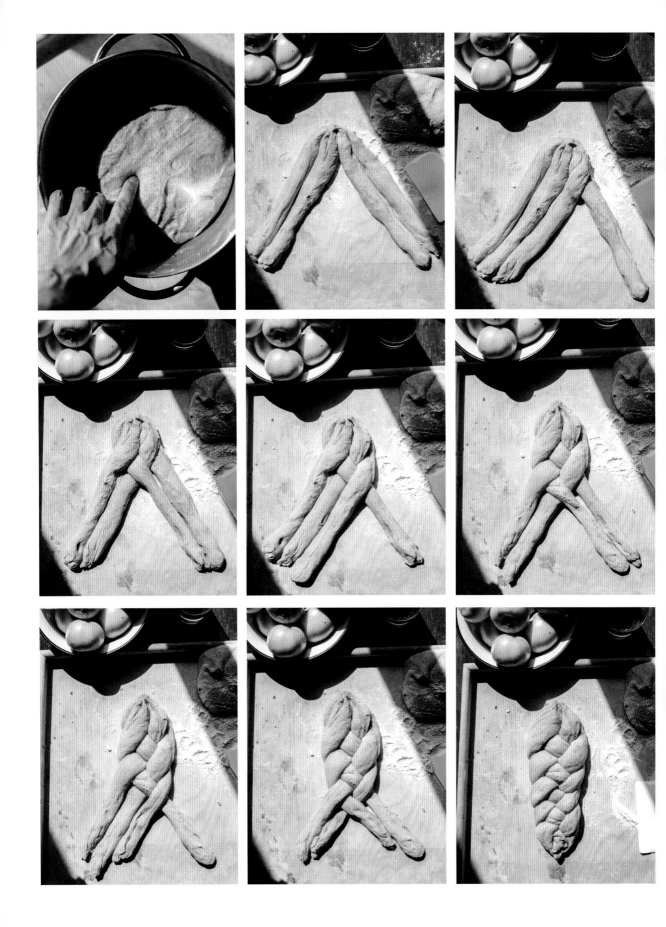

1. **To make the dough,** combine the bread and whole wheat flours, sugar, yeast, and 1 tablespoon salt in the bowl of a stand mixer fitted with a dough hook. In a small bowl, beat together 1 egg and the 2 egg yolks. Add them to the flour mixture along with the melted butter and 1¼ cups (300 ml) lukewarm water. Mix on medium speed for 1 minute. Turn up the speed to medium-high and knead until the dough is soft and silky, about 10 minutes. When you push down, the dough should feel firm and elastic.

2. Transfer the dough to the clean bowl. Cover with plastic wrap and let sit in a warm place until the dough has tripled in volume, about 50 minutes. To test if the dough has fully risen, make an indentation with your finger in the center of the dough. If the indentation remains, move on to the next step. If not, continue to let it rise.

3. While the dough rises, prepare the almond streusel. Whisk together the whole wheat flour, almond flour, sugar, and salt. Add the butter and mix, using your fingers, until the streusel takes on a light bread-crumb texture. Chill in the fridge for at least 30 minutes.

4. Once the dough has risen, separate it into two parts. While you work with one part, keep the other covered with a kitchen towel so it doesn't dry out.

5. **To make a three-stranded challah,** separate the dough into three equal pieces. For a four-stranded challah, separate it into four equal pieces. Roll each piece of dough into a long strand roughly 1 inch (2.5 cm) in diameter.

6. Lay out the strands side by side, running lengthwise away from you, on a clean work surface and squeeze them together only at the very top. For a three-stranded challah, braid the pieces together like braiding hair or yarn: Take the right-most piece over the center, then the left-most piece over the (new) center, and so on. When you reach the end of the braid, squeeze the ends together. For a four-stranded challah, start with the strand farthest to the right and weave it towards the left through the other strands using this pattern: over, under, over. Take the new strand farthest to the right and repeat the weaving pattern again: over, under, over. Repeat this pattern, always starting with the strand farthest to the right, until all the strands are braided. Repeat for the second loaf.

7. Transfer the loaves to a large, parchment paper–lined baking sheet, leaving plenty of space between them. Whisk together the remaining egg, 1 tablespoon water, and a pinch of salt to make an egg wash. Brush the egg wash over the challahs. Sprinkle the streusel topping on top.

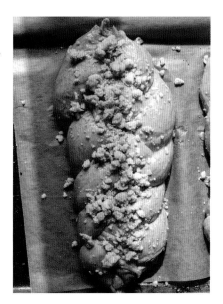

8. Preheat the oven to 350°F (180°C). Place the baking sheet in the middle of the oven and bake for 35 to 40 minutes, or until the loaves are golden. Let them cool on a wire rack.

   Note: Challah keeps very well for several days at room temperature in a bread box or wrapped in a kitchen towel and then a plastic bag. It can also be wrapped well and frozen for up to 3 months. Thaw it slowly, preferably still wrapped, overnight in the refrigerator.

BAKED YEASTED PIEROGI
with Buckwheat, *Twaróg,* and Mint
Krasnobrodzkie pierogi z kaszą gryczaną, twarogiem i miętą

These pierogi are absolutely extraordinary and, at the same time, endearing in their simplicity. This recipe for baked pierogi—essentially stuffed savory buns—comes from my dad's family. He was born in small-town Krasobród, in the beautiful Roztocze region. We used to go there every Christmas, and my grandma would make these pierogi for a late brunch meal. Though no one agreed with her at the time, she liked adding dried mint to the buckwheat-cheese filling. But I think it's a really great idea.

MAKES	PREP TIME	RISING TIME	BAKE TIME
12 buns	30 minutes	1½ hours	35 minutes

FOR THE DOUGH

2½ cups (320 g) all-purpose flour, plus more for shaping

One ¼-ounce (7 g) packet instant yeast

1 tablespoon sugar

½ teaspoon salt

1 large egg

½ cup (120 ml) milk

¼ cup (½ stick/60 g) unsalted butter, melted

FOR THE FILLING

½ cup (100 g) whole buckwheat (kasha)

2 tablespoons (30 g) unsalted butter

1 medium white onion (5 ounces/150 g), chopped

3 garlic cloves, sliced

1 cup (170 g) crumbled farmer cheese or *Twaróg* (page 44)

½ teaspoon dried mint

Salt and freshly ground black pepper

FOR THE EGG WASH

1 large egg

1 tablespoon milk

FOR SERVING

1 tablespoon cold-pressed rapeseed oil

Flaky sea salt

Fresh mint leaves

1. **To make the dough,** combine the flour, yeast, sugar, and salt in the bowl of a stand mixer fitted with a dough hook. Add the egg, milk, and melted butter. Knead on medium-high speed until the dough is soft and silky, about 8 minutes. Cover with a kitchen towel and let rise until it doubles in volume, about 1½ hours. When you push down with your finger, the dough should feel firm and elastic.

2. While the dough rises, make the filling. Boil 1 cup salted water in a medium saucepan. Add the buckwheat and cook, covered, over low heat for 15 minutes, until all the liquid has been absorbed. Remove from the heat and keep covered.

3. Heat the butter in a medium skillet over medium heat. Add the onion and garlic and cook, stirring frequently, until soft, 4 to 5 minutes. Transfer to the pot with the buckwheat. Add the *twaróg* and dried mint and stir to combine. Season with salt and lots of pepper, to taste. Let cool completely.

4. Lightly flour a work surface and turn the dough out onto it. Sprinkle the dough with a little more flour and fold it over onto itself twice. Divide the dough into 12 pieces. Roll out each piece into a 4-inch (10 cm) circle. Place 1 to 2 tablespoons buckwheat filling in the center of each circle, fold the dough over the filling to meet in the center, and pinch the edges to seal.

5. Place the buns, seam side down, on a medium baking sheet covered with parchment paper, leaving them space to rise. Cover with a kitchen towel and let sit in a warm place until noticeably puffy, about 30 minutes.

6. Meanwhile, preheat the oven to 350°F (180°C).

7. **To make the egg wash,** beat the egg and milk together in a small bowl. Gently brush the egg wash over the buns. Bake the buns for 30 to 40 minutes, until golden brown.

8. Remove from the oven and brush with the oil. Sprinkle with sea salt and top with fresh mint leaves. Serve hot.

Note: If you can't find dried mint, mint tea will work perfectly. Cut open a teabag and use it in this recipe. You can also use fresh or dried oregano for a different variation.

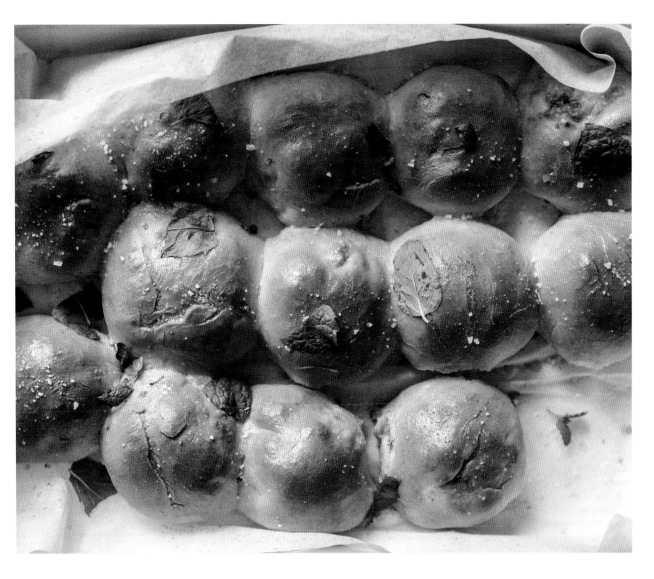

BUTTERMILK PAN BUNS
Proziaki

This is the most characteristic dish from my region, Podkarpacie, in southeastern Poland. These buns are made only with flour, buttermilk or kefir, a bit of salt, and baking soda. Since they are so quick to prepare, they were originally baked when there was no bread available, but they are so delicious that I like to eat them any day of the week. *Proziaki* taste best straight from the pan, served with butter and sea salt flakes or with your favorite preserves.

MAKES	COOK TIME
8 buns	15 minutes

4 cups (520 g) all-purpose flour, plus more for shaping

1½ teaspoons baking soda

1¼ teaspoons kosher salt

1 cup (240 ml) buttermilk or kefir

1. Combine the flour, baking soda, and salt in a large bowl. Add the buttermilk, stirring constantly to form a smooth dough.

2. Sprinkle a work surface with flour and turn out the dough onto it. Divide the dough into 8 equal pieces, then shape them into ovals or squares about ½ inch (1.25 cm) thick.

3. Heat a large cast-iron or nonstick skillet over medium heat. Turn down the heat to medium-low. Place the pieces of dough in the skillet. Cook in batches, if necessary, so the dough pieces don't touch.

4. Cook the buns, uncovered, for 5 to 7 minutes, until the undersides turn golden brown, then flip and cook for 5 to 7 minutes to brown the other side.

5. Transfer the finished buns to a plate or wire rack. Let cool for 5 minutes before serving.

   Note: I recommend eating these buns right away, but you can also store them for up to 2 days at room temperature, wrapped in a kitchen towel.

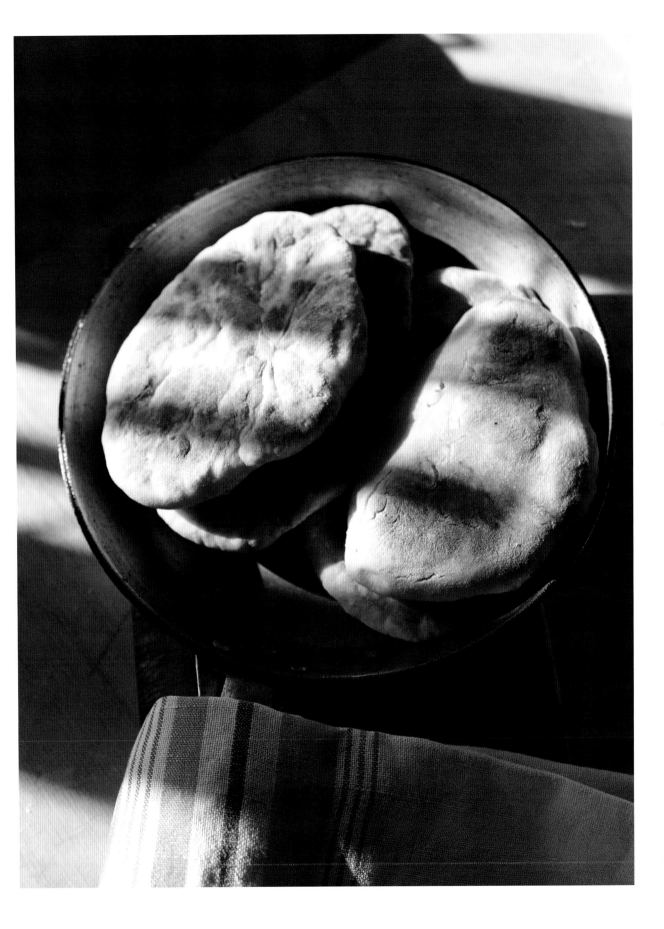

OATMEAL BUNS

Bułeczki na owsiance

I usually start my day with hot oatmeal, a cozy meal for cold, frosty mornings. Sometimes I cook a little extra, to have a few tablespoons to use to make buns. The oatmeal gives these buns their soft texture and helps them stay moist for several days. You can use oatmeal cooked in water or in milk, which gives these buns an even more delicate taste.

MAKES	PREP TIME	RISING TIME	BAKE TIME
12 buns	20 minutes	40 minutes	15 minutes

1 cup (100 g) quick-cooking oats

3 tablespoons (45 g) unsalted butter

4 cups (520 g) all-purpose flour, plus more for shaping

One ¼-ounce (7 g) packet instant yeast

1 teaspoon salt

⅓ cup (30 g) old-fashioned rolled oats, plus more for topping

1 tablespoon honey

Vegetable oil

1 large egg

1. Bring 1½ cups (360 ml) water to a boil; add the quick-cooking oats. Cook, stirring constantly, until thick, about 1 minute. Remove from the heat. Add the butter; stir until melted. Let cool slightly.

2. Combine the flour, yeast, and salt in the bowl of a stand mixer fitted with a dough hook. Add the cooked oatmeal, rolled oats, honey, and 1 cup (240 ml) water. Knead on medium-high speed until the dough is soft and silky, 8 to 10 minutes.

3. Grease a large bowl with oil, then transfer dough to the bowl. Cover with plastic wrap and let sit in a warm place until noticeably puffy, about 1 hour.

4. Preheat the oven to 375°F (190°C). Line a large baking sheet with parchment paper.

5. Turn out the dough onto a floured work surface and divide into 12 equal pieces. Shape each piece into a round bun, with the seam on the bottom. Place the buns, seam side down, on the baking sheet, cover with a kitchen towel, and let rise for 30 to 40 minutes, until they have nearly doubled in volume.

6. Beat the egg with 1 tablespoon water and brush the buns with the egg wash. Top with extra rolled oats. Bake the buns for 15 to 18 minutes, until golden brown. Let cool on a wire rack before serving.

   Note: *Instead of the all-purpose flour, you can use 5 cups (550 g) white spelt flour.*

SOURDOUGH RYE BREAD

Chleb żytni na zakwasie

Sourdough rye is one of the most popular breads in Poland. It is sometimes made with added yeast or wheat flour, which makes the flavor less intense. In my hometown of Rzeszów, there is an old bakery called Nawłoka, where they bake it my favorite way, with just rye flour and *zakwas* (rye sourdough) starter. It has an extremely nutty flavor and a strong, sour punch. My sourdough recipe is an interpretation of this bread—and it's so simple to make. Remember to eat the first slice simply with butter, so you can taste all the flavors with that first bite.

MAKES	PREP TIME	FERMENTING TIME	RISING TIME	BAKE TIME
1 loaf	5 minutes	up to 12 hours	6 hours	50 minutes

FOR THE BREAD STARTER

½ cup (110 g) Sourdough Starter (page 67)

¼ cup (30 g) whole rye flour

¾ cup (90 g) rye flour

¾ cup (180 ml) mineral water

FOR THE BREAD

Unsalted butter

2 cups (220 g) rye flour, plus more for the pan and topping

1 tablespoon salt

2 tablespoons honey

1. **To make the bread starter,** mix the sourdough starter, flours, and water in a medium bowl. Cover with a kitchen towel and leave to ferment at room temperature overnight, 8 to 12 hours, until it bubbles and begins to smell like apple cider vinegar.

2. Lightly butter and flour a 9 x 5-inch (22 x 12 cm) loaf pan.

3. **To make the bread,** add the rye flour, salt, ¾ cup (180 ml) warm water, and the honey to the starter. Stir to combine. Transfer the batter to the loaf pan, dust the top with flour, and cover with a kitchen towel. Let rise at room temperature until it reaches the top edge of the pan, 3 to 6 hours, depending on the age of your starter and the temperature of your kitchen.

4. Preheat the oven to 400°F (200°C). Bake until the crust is dark brown and very well done, about 50 minutes. Remove from the pan, and let cool completely on a wire rack.

   Note: If you prefer a less sour taste, or you are not confident with your starter, add one ¼-ounce (7 g) packet instant yeast with flour to the batter in step 3. Rising will take 1 to 2 hours.

SOURDOUGH STARTER

Zakwas

If you're not lucky enough to have a sourdough starter passed down to you from another home baker, don't be scared. Making your own is easy as pie—or, like bread with butter (*bułka z masłem*), as we say in Poland.

MAKES	PREP TIME	FERMENTING TIME
1½ cups (330 g)	5 minutes	6 days

1¾ cups (245 g) whole rye flour

1¼ cups (140 g) rye flour

1¼ cups (300 ml) mineral water

1. To begin the starter, combine ½ cup (70 g) of the whole rye flour and ½ cup (120 ml) water in a medium glass jar. Cover it loosely with a kitchen towel and let the mixture sit at warm room temperature for 24 hours. After 24 hours, you may see a bit of growth or bubbling.

2. Discard about half the starter and feed the remaining starter, adding ¼ cup (28 g) of the rye flour, ¼ cup (35 g) of the whole rye flour, and ¼ cup (60 ml) of the mineral water. Mix well, cover again with the towel, and let the mixture rest at room temperature for 24 hours.

3. Repeat step 2, continuing to feed the starter for the next 4 days.

4. Once the starter is ready, it should be active, with bubbles breaking the surface.

   Notes: If the starter has any signs of mold, discard it immediately and start again.

   After the starter is ready to use, you can store it in the refrigerator and feed it once a week with a ¼ cup (28 g) rye flour, ¼ cup (35 g) whole rye flour, and ½ cup (120 ml) mineral water. It will last indefinitely as long as you continue to feed it.

SWEET BLUEBERRY BUNS
with Streusel
Jagodzianki

During summer, everyone freaks out about these buns. You can buy them everywhere, and every pastry shop claims they make the best ones. But honestly, homemade *jagodzianki* are even better. Enter these buttery buns, dotted with plenty of blueberries and a touch of sugar. They are so easy to make and insanely delicious. You can fill them with any berries you like.

MAKES	PREP TIME	RESTING TIME	RISING TIME	CHILLING TIME	BAKE TIME
9 buns	30 minutes	12 hours	2 hours	30 minutes	20 minutes

FOR THE DOUGH

2 cups (280 g) all-purpose flour, plus more for shaping

¼ cup (50 g) sugar

1½ teaspoons (5 g) instant yeast

¼ teaspoon kosher salt

1 large egg, lightly beaten

¼ cup (60 ml) milk

6 tablespoons (¾ stick/85 g) unsalted butter, melted

1 tablespoon sour cream

Vegetable oil

FOR THE FILLING

About 1 pound (450 g) blueberries or bilberries

¼ cup (50 g) sugar

3 tablespoons cornstarch

FOR THE STREUSEL

¾ cup (100 g) all-purpose flour

¼ teaspoon salt

¼ cup (50 g) sugar

4 tablespoons (¼ cup/60 g) unsalted butter, chilled and cut into pieces

FOR THE EGG WASH

1 large egg

1 tablespoon milk

1. **To make the dough,** combine the flour, sugar, yeast, and salt in the bowl of a stand mixer fitted with a dough hook. Add the egg, milk, melted butter, and sour cream. Knead at medium-high speed until the dough is soft and silky, about 8 minutes.

2. Grease a large bowl with oil and transfer the dough to it. Cover with plastic wrap and let rest in the fridge for 8 to 12 hours. The dough won't rise much.

3. **To make the filling,** combine the blueberries, sugar, and cornstarch in a medium bowl.

4. Lightly flour a work surface and turn the dough out onto it. Sprinkle the dough with a little more flour and fold it over onto itself twice. Divide the dough into 9 pieces and shape each into a circle about 5 inches (13 cm) in diameter. Place 2 to 3 tablespoons of the blueberry mixture in the center of each circle, fold the dough over the filling to meet in the center, and pinch the edges to seal.

5. Place the buns, seam side down, on a baking sheet covered with a parchment paper, leaving them space to rise. Cover with a kitchen towel and let sit in a warm place until noticeably puffy, about 2 hours.

6. While the buns rest, make the streusel topping. In a medium bowl, whisk together the all-purpose flour and sugar. Add the butter and mix it into the flour, using your fingertips, until the streusel has a light bread-crumb texture. Transfer to the fridge and chill for at least 30 minutes.

7. Preheat the oven to 375°F (190°C).

8. **To make the egg wash,** beat the egg and milk together in a small bowl. Gently brush the buns with the egg wash. Scatter the streusel topping over the buns. Bake until golden brown, 20 to 25 minutes. Cool on a wire rack.

Note: Polish jagodzianki are traditionally stuffed with bilberries (jagody), a small, wild blueberry native to Poland. Use them if you have access to them.

KEFIR CULTURED BUTTER

Masło z kulturami bakterii

All butter is great, but some butter is truly fabulous. Culturing the cream with kefir turns it into tangy, milky crème fraîche, which is just a step away from becoming pure butter (and buttermilk). All heavy cream that's beaten too long will turn into butter, but this one packs a whole new depth of flavor.

MAKES	PREP TIME	FERMENTING TIME	CHILLING TIME
9 ounces (1 generous cup/250 g) butter	20 minutes	8 to 12 hours	1 hour

2 cups (480 g) heavy cream

⅓ cup (80 ml) kefir

¼ teaspoon fine sea salt

1. Pour the heavy cream and kefir into a medium bowl. Whisk briefly to combine, then cover the bowl with a clean kitchen towel. Set in a slightly warm place to culture for 8 to 12 hours, until it smells slightly sour and tangy.

2. Chill the cultured cream in the refrigerator for about 1 hour. Transfer it to the bowl of a stand mixer fitted with a whisk attachment. Cover the top with plastic wrap or a kitchen towel to prevent splattering. Whip until it becomes grainy, about 10 minutes. Let rest for 1 minute, then begin whipping again, until the solid mass (butter) and liquid (buttermilk) have separated, about 5 minutes.

3. Pour off the buttermilk (see Note) and transfer the butter to a clean bowl. Add about ¼ cup (60 ml) cold water and rinse the butter by pressing and folding it. Repeat this two or three times until the water runs just about clear. Discard the rinse water.

4. Sprinkle the salt over the butter and knead it in. Place the butter into a jar with a cover. Store in the fridge up to 3 weeks.

Note: The mixture will splatter heavily in the final stages of churning, so be sure the plastic wrap is secure. The buttermilk will keep for 2 days in the fridge. You can use it to make Buttermilk-Honey French Toast (page 43), Buttermilk Pan Buns (page 60), New Potatoes and Buttermilk Soup (page 85), or Yeast-Buttermilk Cake with Berries and Streusel (page 189).

SOUPS
Zupy

Soups are a huge part of the daily Polish menu. Traditionally, dinner, eaten around 4:00 PM, includes a main dish and a soup that precedes it. Soup is considered a starter, and there are a lot to choose from. Polish cuisine boasts an impressive range of soups for every season and occasion. On hot days, we like to cool down with bright pink *Chłodnik litewski* (Chilled Beet Soup with Cucumbers, Radish, and Dill, page 81), and when we need something filling, we prepare *Żurek* (page 93), a sourdough soup typically made with potatoes, egg, and sausage, or, as in my version, with dried mushrooms.

Soup is also the easiest way to let your fantasies run wild. Just choose the most beautiful seasonal ingredients, prepare a good *Warzywny bulion* (Vegetable Broth, page 77), and you can go crazy with it. Blend it or don't; add cream or leave it plain—there are so many possibilities. That's how I came up with ideas for a few soups that now appear at my table. *Krem z kiszonej kapusty* (Creamy Sauerkraut Soup, page 90) is my variation on the traditional rustic cabbage soup *kapuśniak;* prepared my way, it gains charm and delicateness. My *Krem z młodych ziemniaków i maślanki* (New Potatoes and Buttermilk Soup, page 85), an ode to Polish summer, became a real hit among my friends after I served it at a dinner party. They said the recipe was "enchanted."

There was always soup ready to eat at my childhood home. My mom cooked it in advance. She never wanted me to get hungry after school, while I waited for dinner. My favorite soup of hers was *Ogórkowa* (Dill Pickle Soup with Buttered Potatoes, page 89). This is my favorite soup to make when I need something quick and hearty, to warm me up from the inside.

VEGETABLE BROTH

Warzywny bulion

It might seem basic, but this is the most important soup recipe in this book. Broth is a fundamental base of nearly every soup—but it can be used for so much more. Eat on its own or with pasta, or use this broth—rich in flavor but not too aggressive—in all of the following recipes for guaranteed success.

MAKES	COOK TIME
1½ quarts (1.5 L)	1½ hours

3 tablespoons (45 g) unsalted butter

3 bay leaves

3 whole cloves

1 teaspoon black peppercorns

½ teaspoon allspice berries

1 medium onion, unpeeled, halved through the root

2 whole garlic cloves, peeled

2 medium carrots, halved

3 medium parsley roots or parsnips, halved

1 celery stalk, halved

1½ teaspoons fine sea salt

1. Melt the butter in large pot over medium heat. Cook stirring often, until it starts to turn dark amber, about 5 minutes. Add the bay leaves, cloves, peppercorns, and allspice. Stir occasionally, until fragrant, 1 to 2 minutes.

2. Add the onion, cut side down, to the spiced butter. Add the garlic, carrots, parsley roots, celery, and salt and cook, stirring occasionally, until vegetables begin to brown, 3 to 4 minutes.

3. Add 3 quarts (2.8 L) cold water. Bring to a boil, then reduce the heat and simmer uncovered, stirring occasionally until broth is reduced by half, 1 to 1½ hours.

4. Let the broth cool slightly, then strain through a fine-mesh sieve into a large bowl. Eat with pasta, or use as a base for your favorite soup.

Note: This broth can be made up to 5 days ahead. Keep covered and chilled or frozen for up to 3 months.

CLEAR FERMENTED BEET SOUP
Barszcz czysty czerwony

Barszcz has many faces. Ukrainian borscht is hearty, with lots of vegetables, potatoes, beans, and meat, and *Chłodnik litewski* (Chilled Beet Soup with Cucumbers, Radish, and Dill, page 81) with buttermilk and sour cream is refreshing in the summer. But only one soup can be king: a ruby-colored beet bouillon built with vegetable broth, fermented beet juice, and mushroom consommé. It's sweet, sour, and umami all at the same time. Unlike other types of borscht, it is not whitened with sour cream, so as not to disturb its clear perfection. At Christmas Eve supper, *barszcz* is simply served in a bowl alongside *Uszka z borowikami* (*Uszka* Dumplings with Porcini, page 172), but it's also often sipped as a hot beverage in a cup, with a savory pastry on the side.

MAKES	PREP TIME	FERMENTING TIME	COOK TIME
4 servings	20 minutes	6 days	1½ hours

FOR THE FERMENTED BEETS

2 pounds (900 g) beets, peeled and sliced

4 garlic cloves

1 bay leaf

2 black peppercorns

1 tablespoon salt

About 3 cups (720 ml) mineral water

FOR THE SOUP

1½ quarts (1½ L) Vegetable Broth (page 77) or water

2 pounds (900 g) beets, peeled and halved

2 whole cloves

1 star anise pod

3 allspice berries

½ teaspoon black peppercorns

3 bay leaves

1 ounce (30 g) dried porcini mushrooms

5 smoked plums (see page 9)

1 tablespoon soy sauce

2 cups (500 ml) juice from the fermented beet (see above)

Red wine vinegar

Salt and freshly ground black pepper

1. **To make the fermented beets,** place the beets into a clean large jar with a lid. Add the garlic cloves, bay leaf, peppercorns, and salt. Pour enough of the mineral water into the jar to completely cover the beets.

2. Screw on the lid and let the jar sit at room temperature until foam starts to appear on top, about 6 days. Discard the foam. Store in the refrigerator; this will keep for several weeks.

3. **To make the soup,** bring the vegetable broth to a boil in a large pot with the beets, cloves, star anise, allspice, peppercorns, and bay leaves. Cook until the beets are soft, 1 to 1½ hours. Strain the liquid and discard the spices and beets (or save the beets for another use—for example, Baked Beet, Apple, and *Bundz* Salad, page 131).

4. Meanwhile, in a medium saucepan, pour enough water over the mushrooms and plums, just to cover them (2 to 3 cups). Cook over low heat until soft, about 30 minutes. Discard the mushrooms and plums, or save them for another use, such as *Uszka* Dumplings with Porcini (page 172).

5. Add the mushroom liquid, soy sauce, and juice from the fermented beet to the soup. Heat through, being careful not to boil it. Season with salt, pepper, and vinegar.

Notes: You can use the leftover mushrooms to make the filling for Uszka *Dumplings with Porcini (page 172).*

Leftover fermented beets work perfectly in salads, with arugula, goat cheese, and honey dressing, for example. You can also slice the beets and add them to sandwiches to give them an extra punch.

CHILLED BEET SOUP
with Cucumbers, Radish, and Dill
Chłodnik litewski

Chilled beet soup, swirled with a wooden spoon, is one of the quiet rewards of hot, lazy midsummer lunches. The trick to making it hearty enough is to not skimp on the seasonings and be patient with chopping to create the right chunky textures. Garlic, dill, chives, and a lot of freshly ground black pepper add plenty of flavor, while buttermilk and sour cream contribute a creamy, light texture. You could serve this on its own, but boiled eggs with runny yolks and some freshly cooked potatoes fill out the meal very nicely.

MAKES	PREP TIME	COOK TIME	CHILLING TIME
4 servings	15 minutes	30 minutes	2 hours

1½ pounds (675 g) beets with greens (about 4 medium beets)

1 teaspoon sugar

3 medium Kirby cucumbers, peeled and coarsely grated

5 radishes, trimmed and chopped into ½-inch (1.25 cm) pieces

2 cups (500 ml) full-fat buttermilk or kefir

1¼ cups (300 ml) sour cream

3 tablespoons chopped fresh dill

3 tablespoons chopped fresh chives

2 garlic cloves, minced

4 medium-boiled eggs, peeled and halved, for serving (optional)

5 or 6 medium Yukon Gold potatoes, cooked and chopped, for serving (optional)

Salt and freshly ground black pepper

1. Using a large knife, separate the greens and stems from the beets. Wash the greens and stems and roughly chop them; set aside. Scrub the beets and cut into ¼-inch (6 mm) chunks.

2. Bring 4 cups (1 L) water to a boil in a large pot with the sugar and ½ teaspoon salt. Add the beets and cook for 20 minutes on medium heat, or until fork-tender. Add the beet greens and stems after 15 minutes to lightly wilt, then drain, reserving 1 cup of the cooking liquid.

3. In a large bowl, gently stir together the cooked beets, greens, and stems with half of the cucumbers and radishes, the buttermilk, sour cream, 2 tablespoons of the dill, 2 tablespoons of the chives, the garlic, and the reserved cooking water. Season with salt and a lot of pepper. Chill the soup for at least 2 hours.

4. To serve, divide the soup among bowls. Top with remaining the cucumbers, radishes, chives, and dill. Divide the eggs and potatoes among the bowls, if desired.

   Note: This soup will keep for 2 days in the fridge in a covered container. Add the garnishes when serving.

TOMATO-APPLE SOUP
with "Poured Noodles"
Pomidorówka z lanymi kluskami

This was my favorite soup growing up, as is probably true for most Poles. An old-fashioned way to cook it involves only tomato paste, chicken stock, sour cream, and flour to thicken it. My grandma used to add an obscene amount of cream, so much that the soup would turn a lovely shade of pink. She also served it with *lane kluski,* "poured noodles." To make them, egg batter is poured straight into boiling water. After a second in the bath, they turn into a soft, light hybrid of noodles and dumplings.

MAKES	PREP TIME	COOK TIME
4 servings	5 minutes	15 minutes

FOR THE SOUP

2 tablespoons (30 g) unsalted butter

2 whole garlic cloves, peeled

1 tablespoon dried marjoram

One 15-ounce (450 g) can crushed tomatoes

1 medium Gala apple (about 7 ounces/200 g), peeled, cored, and chopped

2 cups (500 ml) Vegetable Broth (page 77)

1 tablespoon tomato paste

3 tablespoons sour cream

Salt and freshly ground black pepper

FOR THE POURED NOODLES

2 large eggs

2 tablespoons sour cream

Salt

6 to 8 tablespoons (100 to 150 g) all-purpose flour

1. **To make the soup,** heat the butter in a medium pot over medium heat. Add the garlic and marjoram and cook, stirring occasionally, until fragrant, 1 minute.

2. Add the tomatoes, apple, broth, and tomato paste, and bring to a boil. Reduce the heat and simmer, stirring occasionally, until the apple softens, 10 to 15 minutes.

3. Remove from the heat and use an immersion blender or transfer to a blender to purée the mixture until smooth. If using a stand blender, transfer the soup back to the pot.

4. Combine about ¼ cup (60 ml) of the hot soup with the sour cream in a small bowl, then add the mixture back into the soup pot. Season with salt and pepper.

5. While the soup is simmering, make the noodles: Whisk together the eggs. sour cream, and a pinch of salt in a medium bowl. Whisk in the flour, 1 tablespoon at a time, until the mixture resembles a sticky dough.

6. Boil water with a pinch of salt in a medium saucepan. Dip a teaspoon into the hot water and use it to drop a small amount of batter into the water. Continue with the rest of the batter and boil the noodles gently until they rise to the top of the water, about 1 minute. Use a slotted spoon or small sieve to transfer the noodles to a plate as they become ready.

7. To serve, divide the soup among bowls. Top with the noodles and season with pepper.

   Note: It's not un-Polish to skip the poured noodles—so if you want to, you can also serve this soup with white rice.

NEW POTATOES AND BUTTERMILK SOUP

Krem z młodych ziemniaków i maślanki

New potatoes with butter and dill, served with a glass of chilled buttermilk, are a beloved summer comfort food in the Polish countryside. Having spent many afternoons enjoying this satisfying combination, I got to daydreaming about a soup version, and here we are. Though it's extremely creamy, there's a tangy punch thanks to the black pepper and buttermilk. Fresh dill makes this soup even more authentic, so don't skip it.

MAKES	PREP TIME	COOK TIME
4 servings	15 minutes	15 minutes

2 tablespoons (30 g) unsalted butter

1 medium onion, chopped

1 garlic clove, sliced

1½ pounds (675 g) new potatoes, peeled and chopped

3¼ cups (775 ml) Vegetable Broth (page 77)

1 cup (240 ml) buttermilk

Chopped fresh dill, for serving

Salt and freshly ground black pepper

1. Heat the butter in a large pot over medium heat. Add the onion and garlic, along with a pinch of salt. Cook, stirring occasionally, until the onion is translucent, 3 to 4 minutes.

2. Add the potatoes and fry, stirring occasionally, until they begin to stick to the pot and turn golden, about 5 minutes.

3. Add the vegetable broth and cook until potatoes are softened, 15 to 20 minutes.

4. Remove from the heat and cool slightly. Transfer to a blender (in batches if necessary), then add the buttermilk and purée until smooth. Season with more salt and pepper. Top each bowl with at least 1 tablespoon dill, and serve.

BARLEY SOUP
with Roasted Veggies
Krupnik z pieczonych warzyw i pęczaku

In many Polish kitchens, *krupnik* is a hearty soup made with a meaty stock and grains, but my version is filled with roasted veggies that give it just as much flavor. I love chewy pearl barley in this soup, but buckwheat, cottage barley, or millet will work here, too.

MAKES	PREP TIME	1 HOUR
6 servings	10 minutes	1 hour

3 medium carrots (about 12 ounces/350 g total), peeled and cut into ½-inch (1.25 cm) pieces

3 medium parsley roots (see Notes) or parsnips (about 12 ounces/350 g total), peeled and cut into ½-inch (1.25 cm) pieces

3 celery stalks, cut into ½-inch (1.25 cm) pieces

1 onion, unpeeled, halved through the root end

3 garlic cloves, unpeeled

1 fresh rosemary sprig

3 bay leaves

¾ teaspoon black peppercorns

¼ to ½ teaspoon allspice berries

3 tablespoons rapeseed, canola, or sunflower oil

½ cup (100 g) pearl barley

⅓ cup (80 ml) heavy cream

Salt and freshly ground black pepper

1. Preheat the oven to 450°F (230°C). Toss the carrots, parsley roots, onion, garlic, rosemary, bay leaves, peppercorns, and allspice with the oil on a rimmed baking sheet. Season with salt. Roast, tossing occasionally, until tender and browned, about 35 minutes.

2. While the vegetables roast, cook the barley. Bring 1½ cups (360 ml) water to a boil. Season with salt and add the barley. Cook, covered, over low heat until all the liquid has been absorbed, about 30 minutes.

3. Transfer the roasted vegetables, spices, and barley to a large pot. Add 2 quarts (2 L) water and bring to a boil. Simmer for about 20 minutes, until the soup is deeply brown. Discard the onion, garlic, and bay leaves. Stir in the cream. Season with salt and ground pepper.

Notes: To give this soup a more developed taste, I don't discard the spices. Make sure to inform your guests about these little surprises before serving.

Parsley root is commonly used in Polish cooking, mainly to prepare perfect broths and soups. I love roasting it to develop a sweeter flavor and then the possibilities are endless. You can eat it as an appetizer or a salad ingredient, or use it to give soups a deeper flavor. If you cannot find parsley root, try parsnip.

DILL PICKLE SOUP
with Buttered Potatoes
Ogórkowa

This tart soup based on dill pickles was one of my favorite things my mother made when I was a child. It's pretty normal for Polish kids to like sour food—acidic flavor is in our veins. If you want a more delicate taste, add the heavy cream. I particularly like adding boiled potatoes with butter. They have a subtle, creamy flavor, and they melt in the mouth.

MAKES	PREP TIME	COOK TIME
4 servings	5 minutes	20 minutes

3 or 4 russet potatoes (about 300 g total), peeled and chopped

¼ cup (½ stick/60 g) unsalted butter

2 garlic cloves, thinly sliced

3 bay leaves

8 ounces (230 g) kosher dill pickles, preferably half-sour, or Salt-Brined Dill Pickles (page 231), chopped (about 1½ cups)

4 cups (1 L) Vegetable Broth (page 77)

3 tablespoons chopped fresh dill, plus more for serving

⅓ cup heavy cream (optional)

Salt and freshly ground black pepper

1. Boil the potatoes in salted water with 2 tablespoons of the butter. Cook until softened, about 20 minutes. Drain the potatoes, reserving 1 cup of the cooking water.

2. Heat the remaining 2 tablespoons butter in a large pot over medium-high heat. Add the garlic and bay leaves and cook until fragrant, about 30 seconds. Add the pickles. Cover the pot and cook for about 15 minutes, until the pickles soften a bit.

3. Add the broth, cooked potatoes, reserved potato cooking water, and dill. Bring to a simmer to heat everything. Season with pepper (the soup should already be very salty). If desired, add heavy cream for a more delicate taste.

4. To serve, divide the soup among bowls and top with more dill.

Notes: For this soup, you will need real Polish-style pickled cucumbers. You can make your own (page 231) or buy them in Polish delis.

Ogórkowa tastes excellent with Onion–Poppy Seed Buns (page 51).

CREAMY SAUERKRAUT SOUP

Krem z kiszonej kapusty

English is not my first language, but even in Polish it's hard for me to put my love for this soup into words. It's perfect. One of a kind. Full of nuanced flavor but with nothing complicated about it. Don't be afraid of the heavy cream alongside the otherwise light ingredients—it tones down the flavor with fermented, tangy, bright notes and gives the whole thing a more delicate taste.

MAKES	PREP TIME	COOK TIME
4 servings	10 minutes	2½ hours

1 pound (3¼ cups/450 g) Sauerkraut (page 232)

2 tablespoons (30 g) unsalted butter

2 shallots, chopped

1 teaspoon ground caraway seeds,

2 medium Yukon Gold potatoes (about 8 ounces/240 g total), peeled and chopped

4 cups (1 L) Vegetable Broth (page 77)

1 cup (240 ml) heavy cream

Salt and freshly ground black pepper

Slivered almonds (optional)

1. Squeeze the liquid from the sauerkraut and reserve it for later. Chop the sauerkraut finely.

2. Heat the butter in a medium pot. Add the shallots and cook, stirring often, until softened, about 3 minutes. Add the caraway and potatoes; cook until fragrant, 1 to 2 minutes.

3. Add the chopped sauerkraut, vegetable broth, and heavy cream. Cook over low heat until potatoes and sauerkraut start to fall apart, about 2 hours.

4. Transfer to a blender (in batches if necessary) or use an immersion blender in the pot to blend the soup until smooth, 1 to 2 minutes. Season with salt, pepper, and up to ¼ cup (60 ml) of the reserved sauerkraut liquid. Serve topped with slivered almonds, if desired.

ŻUREK WITH DRIED PORCINI

Wegetariański żurek z borowikami

Żurek is the most extraordinary Polish dish. The base of this soup is a special rye sourdough *żur*, a fermented mixture of flour and water, which makes it sour, salty, and creamy. *Żurek* is unlike almost anything else. It can be delicate and brothy or hearty, stuffed with chunks of kielbasa and potatoes—even served in a bread bowl, which soaks up the flavors from the soup. My version is packed with dried porcini, which add another level of umami. I think it's fun to have an egg with a runny yolk in my soup, and you should, too!

MAKES	FERMENTING TIME	PREP TIME	COOK TIME
4 servings	5 days	80 minutes	80 minutes

FOR THE *ŻUR* (SEE NOTE)

½ cup (55g) whole rye flour

2-inch (5 cm) crust from Sourdough Rye Bread (page 64)

1 garlic clove

2 cups (480 ml) warm mineral water

FOR THE SOUP

1 cup (40 g) dried mushrooms, preferably porcini

4 cups (960 ml) Vegetable Broth (page 77)

1½ cups (360 ml) *żur*

1 tablespoon dried marjoram

½ cup (120 ml) heavy cream

Salt and freshly ground black pepper

FOR SERVING

4 boiled potatoes, hot

4 soft-boiled eggs, peeled and halved

Chopped fresh parsley

1. **To make the *żur*,** place the flour, bread crust, garlic, and mineral water in a 1-quart (1 L) jar. Cover with a kitchen towel. Leave to ferment at room temperature for 5 days. Stir once a day.

2. **To make the soup,** soak the dried mushrooms in 3 cups water in a large pot for 1 hour. Bring to a boil, then cook over low heat, until soft, 50 to 60 minutes. Discard the bread and garlic.

3. Add the vegetable broth, *żur*, and marjoram. Bring to a boil; cook until it thickens a bit, about 10 minutes. Stir in the heavy cream. Remove from heat. Season with salt and pepper.

4. To serve, divide the soup among four bowls. Add the potatoes and eggs. Top with parsley.

   Note: In Poland, żur is available in bottles at every supermarket. Abroad, you can find it in Polish delis or online. You can use 1½ cups (360 ml) store-bought żur here instead of making your own.

ALMOND SOUP
with Floating Clouds
Migdałowa zupa "nic"

The almond soup is a holiday version of Polish "nothing" soup (*zupa nic*). It refers to the tough times when our grandmothers didn't have much to eat—only a few eggs, some milk, and a little sugar. It sounds like a dessert, but it's usually served as breakfast or *podwieczorek,* a sweet meal between lunch and supper. This indulgent recipe is served with puffy clouds of softly poached meringue floating on top and sprinkled with a pinch of cinnamon that warms from the inside of the soul.

MAKES	PREP TIME	COOK TIME
4 to 6 servings	15 minutes	10 minutes

FOR THE SOUP

2 cups (480 ml) milk

½ cup (120 ml) heavy cream

½ teaspoon ground cinnamon, plus more for serving

2 tablespoons honey

¼ (30 g) cup ground almonds

¼ teaspoon salt

¼ cup (30 g) slivered almonds, for serving (optional)

FOR THE CLOUDS

2 egg whites

Pinch of salt

¼ cup (50 g) sugar

1. **To make the soup,** combine the milk, cream, cinnamon, honey, ground almonds, and salt in a medium saucepan. Bring to a boil, then cook over low heat for 5 to 10 minutes, until slightly thickened. Remove from the heat.

2. Meanwhile, make the clouds. Place the egg whites in a clean mixing bowl with the salt. Whip the whites until stiff, then add the sugar in two rounds; continue beating until shiny peaks form.

3. Bring 3 cups water to a simmer in a wide skillet. Spoon the whites into cloud shapes and lower them into the simmering water. Cover the pan and cook for about 5 minutes, until the clouds are firm. Remove with a slotted spoon.

4. To serve, divide the soup among shallow bowls. Top each with clouds. Garnish with a pinch of cinnamon and almonds, if desired.

Note: The soup can be served lukewarm or chilled.

MAIN DISHES
Dania główne

Nowadays, Polish cuisine is very meat heavy, but it hasn't always been that way. Until fairly recently, meat was a luxury that only the richest could afford. (It's crazy how history can change the way people eat.) But even magnates and aristocrats didn't eat it all the time since, in our Catholic country, people fasted long and often. They did eat fish and seafood, because—though I don't understand why—they weren't considered meat. Vegetarian dishes began to appear in Polish cookbooks as early as the seventeenth century, and the first documented vegetarian recipe is *ćwikła* (beetroot salad with horseradish), by the poet Mikołaj Rej in "The Life of the Honest Man" in 1567.

In Poland, it isn't difficult to cook a delicious, wholesome meal without meat. There are so many popular varieties of beans and grains—buckwheat, millet, pearl barley—and fresh seasonal vegetables are sold at farmers markets around all the cities. I like to go to my favorite markets, Hala Banacha or Mirowska, the culinary heart of Warsaw, and choose the ingredients that look most beautiful. In autumn, when the stalls are full of orange pumpkins and zucchini, I use them to prepare *Soczewicowe leczo* (Lentil, Butternut Squash, and Zucchini Stew, page 105) with smoked paprika; as spring comes I cannot tear myself away from the surprisingly light *Kaszotto ze szparagami, cydrem i kozim serem* (Barley Risotto with Asparagus, Cider, and Goat Cheese, page 111). I never forget, especially in winter, about one of my favorite polish dishes—*Bigos z wędzonym śliwkami i soczewicą* (*Bigos* with Smoked Plums and Lentils, page 112), made with fresh and fermented cabbage and lots of spices. Polish food is all about the comfort and joy that it brings.

SAUERKRAUT FRITTERS

Fuczki

Fuczki are fried like *Placki ziemniaczane* (Potato Fritters with Rosemary and Horseradish Sauce, page 119), but made with sauerkraut. The most important ingredient is good, naturally pickled cabbage. First, the sauerkraut should be well drained, then chopped and mixed with the batter. The pancakes that result are tangy, crispy on the outside but pleasantly chewy on the inside, just like the ones I used to eat during family trips to the Bieszczady mountains, where they come from.

MAKES	COOK TIME
8 to 12 fritters	15 minutes

10½ ounces (2 cups/300 g) Sauerkraut (page 232), well drained

¾ cup (190 ml) milk

1 large egg, lightly beaten

1 teaspoon caraway seeds

1 teaspoon dried savory (optional)

1 cup (130 g) all-purpose flour

Salt and freshly ground black pepper

Canola oil or clarified butter

1. Finely chop the sauerkraut. In a medium bowl, mix the milk, egg, caraway seeds, and savory, if using. Stir in the flour. Season with salt and pepper. Add the sauerkraut and mix to combine.

2. Heat a thin layer of oil in a large skillet over medium heat, until a small amount of batter added to the fat sizzles and sputters. Working in batches, spoon 2 tablespoons of the sauerkraut mixture per fritter into the pan (you should be able to fit about four at a time). Spread them into 3-inch (8 cm) rounds with a fork. Cook until the undersides are browned, about 5 minutes. Turn the fritters over and cook until the other sides are browned, about 5 minutes more.

3. Transfer to paper towels to drain and season with salt. Repeat with the remaining batter, adding more oil to the pan as needed. Serve hot.

   Note: Serve fuczki *by themselves, with sour cream and parsley, or as a side dish to* Fasolka po bretońsku *(Breton Beans with Dried Tomatoes, page 102).*

BRETON BEANS
with Dried Tomatoes
Fasolka po bretońsku

This beloved Polish classic is traditionally made with sausage, but I usually don't have any in my fridge. So I switch the meat out for sun-dried tomatoes and smoked paprika—a trick I've come to love more than the original. *Fasolka po bretońsku* is one of the quickest dinners to make after a long, cold day. There is something so cozy about the way the kitchen fills with the scent of spices, and about the softness of the beans, which melt in your mouth.

MAKES	PREP TIME	COOK TIME
4 servings	5 minutes	25 minutes

2 tablespoons (30 g) unsalted butter

1 medium white onion, chopped

3 bay leaves

2 allspice berries

¼ teaspoon black peppercorns

1 teaspoon dried marjoram

¾ teaspoon smoked sweet paprika

½ teaspoon sweet paprika

Two 15-ounce (425 g) cans cannellini beans, drained

½ cup (100 g) sun-dried tomatoes in oil, drained and chopped

One 15-ounce (425 g) can crushed tomatoes

1 tablespoon tomato paste

Sugar

Salt and freshly ground black pepper

1. Melt the butter in large pot over medium heat. Add the onion and season with salt. Cook, stirring occasionally, until translucent, about 3 minutes. Add the bay leaves, allspice, peppercorns, marjoram, and smoked and sweet paprikas. Stir occasionally until fragrant, 1 to 2 minutes.

2. Add the beans, sun-dried and crushed tomatoes, tomato paste, and 1 cup water. Cook until the beans are soft and the flavors have combined, about 15 minutes. Season with pepper, salt, and sugar.

3. Divide the beans among four bowls. Serve with slices of Sourdough Rye Bread (page 64) and butter.

LENTIL, BUTTERNUT SQUASH, AND ZUCCHINI STEW

Soczewicowe leczo

In Poland, the autumn chill sets in the first days of October, but there is still plenty of fresh produce to enjoy. Sweet tomatoes, bright green zucchini, and the first beautiful winter squash displayed on farmers market tables are just begging to be used in this cozy stew. Squash works really well with lentils, making a hearty base infused with aromatic vegetables. I particularly like the way the sweet flavor and comforting, creamy texture of the butternut squash plays against the strong flavors of smoked paprika, which raises this vegetarian stew to a new level.

MAKES	PREP TIME	COOK TIME
4 servings	10 minutes	30 minutes

3 tablespoons sunflower oil

1 medium white onion, diced

⅔ cup green or red lentils

¼ cup dry apple cider (optional)

1 pound (450 g) butternut squash, peeled and chopped

3 medium zucchini, cubed (about 4 cups/680 g)

1½ cups (360 ml) Vegetable Broth (page 77)

2 pounds (900 g) tomatoes, chopped, or two 14-ounce cans crushed tomatoes

1 teaspoon smoked sweet paprika

½ teaspoon cayenne pepper

Salt and freshly ground black pepper

1. Heat oil in a large pot over medium heat. Add the onion and season with salt. Cook, stirring occasionally, until translucent, 3 to 4 minutes.

2. Add the lentils and stir for 1 minute. Add the cider, if using, and wait until it has evaporated, about 30 seconds. Add the butternut squash and zucchini and stir for 3 minutes. Add the vegetable broth and tomatoes. Season with the paprika, cayenne, salt, and pepper.

3. Cook until the vegetables are softened, 15 to 20 minutes. Season with more salt and black pepper and serve hot. Serve with freshly baked bread and butter.

   Note: This stew will improve if it rests overnight. It keeps well for 3 or 4 days—though you will probably finish it sooner.

POTATO-BUCKWHEAT *GOŁĄBKI*
with Tomato-Vodka Sauce
Gołąbki z ziemniakami i kaszą (Hołubicie)

The most popular *gołąbki* (stuffed cabbage rolls) contain rice and minced meat. There are also variations with groats or potatoes, or both—like in this recipe. Mashed potatoes are enriched with cooked buckwheat, *twaróg,* and rosemary for an earthy flavor. This filling is amazingly soft and fluffy and nearly melts in the mouth. For a sharper taste, I prepare the tomato sauce with Polish bison grass vodka, which has a nice herbaceous flavor. Serve these delicate cabbage rolls with a crunchy, nutty topping of *Popcorn z kaszy gryczanej* (Popped Buckwheat, page 236).

MAKES	PREP TIME	COOK TIME
4 to 6 servings	50 minutes	30 minutes

FOR THE CABBAGE ROLLS

⅔ cup (130 g) whole buckwheat (kasha)

1 pound (450 g) medium russet potatoes, peeled and chopped

1 cup (200 g) farmer cheese or *Twaróg* (page 44), plus more for serving

2 tablespoons (30 g) unsalted butter

1 large white onion (7 ounces/200 g), chopped

3 garlic cloves, minced

1 teaspoon chopped fresh rosemary

1 medium head savoy cabbage (about 2 pounds/900 g)

Popped Buckwheat (page 236)

Salt and freshly ground black pepper

TOMATO-VODKA SAUCE

3 tablespoons (45 g) unsalted butter

1 medium onion (5 ounces/150 g), chopped

3 garlic cloves, minced

1 teaspoon chopped fresh rosemary

3 tablespoons tomato paste

¼ cup (60 ml) bison grass vodka

One 14-ounce (400 g) can crushed tomatoes

½ cup (120 ml) heavy cream

recipe continues . . .

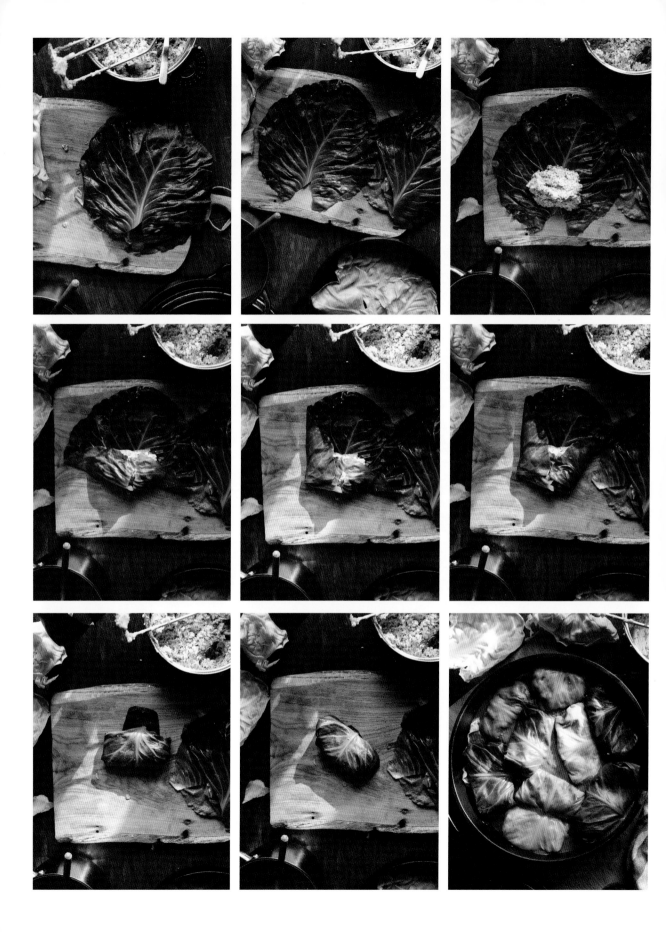

1. **To make the stuffed cabbage,** boil 1⅓ cups salted water in a medium saucepan. Add the buckwheat and cook, covered, over low heat for 15 minutes, until all liquid has been absorbed. Remove from the heat and leave covered.

2. Boil the potatoes in generously salted water until soft, 15 to 20 minutes, then drain. Mash the potatoes, add the *twaróg,* and mash again. Stir in the cooked buckwheat.

3. Heat the butter in a medium skillet over medium heat. Add the onion; cook, stirring occasionally, until soft, about 5 minutes. Add the garlic and rosemary; cook until fragrant, about 1 minute. Stir the cooked onion into the potato-buckwheat mixture. Season with salt and pepper.

4. Boil enough water to cover the cabbage in a large pot. Add the cabbage, and cook, until leaves are soft, about 10 minutes. Remove the cabbage from the water and drain. Remove 10 to 12 whole leaves from the cabbage head, cutting out any thick tough center ribs.

5. Preheat the oven to 350°F (180°C). Place 3 heaping tablespoons of the filling on each cabbage leaf. Fold the right side of the leaf into the middle, then fold in the left side. Fold the bottom of the leaf up and over, and you will have something that looks like an envelope. Roll the leaf away from you to encase the filling and make a neat little roll. Cover the bottom of a casserole dish with remaining leaves. (I like to use the uglier ones here.) Place the cabbage rolls tightly in the dish.

6. **To make the sauce,** heat the butter in a medium saucepan. Add the onion and cook, stirring occasionally, until soft, 4 to 5 minutes. Add the garlic and rosemary; cook for 30 seconds. Add the tomato paste and cook, stirring occasionally until the paste is deep red and starting to brown on the bottom of the pot, 5 to 6 minutes. Add the vodka and stir to incorporate, scraping the bottom of the pot. Add the crushed tomatoes with their juices and bring to a boil. Blend the mixture with an immersion blender, then stir in the heavy cream. Season with salt and pepper.

7. Pour the sauce over the cabbage rolls. Bake until soft, 15 to 20 minutes.

8. To serve, divide the cabbage rolls among plates. Top with Popped Buckwheat (page 236) and *twaróg.*

BARLEY RISOTTO
with Asparagus, Cider, and Goat Cheese
Kaszotto ze szparagami, cydrem i kozim serem

Risotto with Polish pearl barley is much simpler to prepare than the classic Italian version with rice. You do not need to stir the pot constantly like an Italian grandma, watching to see if another cup of broth is needed. Instead, you simply cook barley in a saucepan (you can even make it a day or two ahead), and use it to prepare a fast, comforting, light dish in around 10 minutes. This *kaszotto* is full of spring asparagus, complemented perfectly by dry apple cider, which is a great replacement for wine. A healthy dollop of soft goat cheese melts and coats every grain of barley. Don't forget to serve it with a glass of chilled cider on the side.

MAKES	COOK TIME
4 servings	30 minutes

3 cups (720 ml) Vegetable Broth (page 77)

1 cup (200 g) pearl barley

3 tablespoons (45 g) unsalted butter

1 large onion (7 ounces/200 g), chopped

3 garlic cloves, thinly sliced

1 bunch (1 pound/450 g) asparagus, trimmed, cut into 1-inch (2.5 cm) pieces

1 cup (240 ml) dry apple cider, plus more if needed

½ teaspoon grated lemon zest

½ cup grated Parmesan cheese, plus more for serving

2 tablespoons soft goat cheese, plus more for serving

Salt and freshly ground black pepper

1. Boil the broth in a large saucepan. Stir in the barley; cook, covered, over low heat until the liquid has been mostly absorbed, 20 to 30 minutes. Remove from the heat; let sit in the covered saucepan.

2. Heat the butter in a large saucepan over medium. Add the onion and cook, stirring frequently, until nearly soft, about 2 minutes. Add the garlic and asparagus; cook until slightly golden brown, about 2 minutes. Remove and set aside the tips of the asparagus from the saucepan. (You will use them for serving.)

3. Stir in the cooked barley. Add the cider; bring to a simmer, and cook over high heat, stirring frequently, until the barley absorbs the liquid, 2 to 3 minutes. Stir in the lemon zest, Parmesan, and goat cheese. Season with salt and pepper. Add more cider for a looser consistency.

4. To serve, divide among plates. Arrange the asparagus tips over the *kaszotto*. Top with more Parmesan and goat cheese. Serve with chilled cider on the side.

Note: This spring risotto also tastes great with other green vegetables, such as English peas, sugar snap peas, or green beans.

BIGOS
with Smoked Plums and Lentils
Bigos z wędzonymi śliwkami i soczewicą

This is one of those rare dishes that is best made a few days in advance, because *bigos* only gets tastier with each reheating. My mom always says you should reheat it at least three times before serving. During the winter, I usually make a big pot of this to eat for a few days, and the last serving is always the best. Don't be scared by the long ingredient list—it's actually very easy, as long as you add the components at the right time. Building the richness here is very important, as this version is meat-free. Lots of spices, good sauerkraut, apple, dry wine, and smoked plums (see page 9) are my little secrets to achieve extraordinary umami.

MAKES	PREP TIME	COOK TIME
4 to 6 servings	10 minutes	4 hours

2 tablespoons (30 g) unsalted butter

1 medium white onion (5 ounces/150 g), thinly sliced

4 bay leaves

4 allspice berries

3 whole cloves

½ teaspoon caraway seeds

½ teaspoon smoked sweet paprika

½ teaspoon sweet paprika

½ teaspoon dried savory or thyme

½ teaspoon dried marjoram

½ teaspoon coriander seeds

½ teaspoon mustard seeds

1 pound (3 cups/450 g) Sauerkraut (page 232), drained and chopped

5 cups (1.25 L) Vegetable Broth (page 77) or water

One 1-pound (450 g) head green cabbage, cored and chopped

1 medium apple (8 ounces/250 g), preferably Granny Smith, cored and grated on the large holes of a box grater

½ cup (75 g) smoked plums, chopped

½ cup (20 g) dried mushrooms

1 teaspoon tomato paste

¼ cup (50 g) green lentils

½ cup (120 ml) dry red wine

1 teaspoon honey

Chopped fresh dill, for serving

Salt and freshly ground black pepper

1. Heat the butter in a large Dutch oven or other large pot over medium heat. Add the onion and cook, stirring often, until softened, about 3 minutes. Add the bay leaves, allspice, cloves, caraway, smoked and sweet paprikas, savory, marjoram, coriander seeds, and mustard seeds and cook until fragrant, 1 to 2 minutes. Add the sauerkraut, 1½ teaspoons salt, and 3 cups of the broth. Bring to a simmer and cook until the sauerkraut has softened, about 40 minutes.

2. Add the cabbage, apple, plums, mushrooms, tomato paste, lentils, wine, honey, and the remaining 2 cups broth. Bring to a simmer. Cover, reduce heat, and simmer gently, stirring a few times, for 3 hours, until everything is softened. Season with salt and pepper.

3. To serve, divide *bigos* among bowls and top with dill. Serve with freshly baked bread and butter.

Note: Bigos can be made 1 week ahead; the flavor will improve as time goes on. Store it covered in the refrigerator.

STUFFED TOMATOES
with Millet, Cinnamon, and Almonds
Faszerowane pomidory z kaszą jaglaną, cynamonem i migdałami

I truly love Polish summer for its sweet tomatoes, which I eat sautéed or simply sprinkled with flaky sea salt. My favorites are large, bulky, and incredibly juicy—they're perfect for stuffing. This slightly sweet filling with a millet base, flavored with cinnamon and dried apricots, is a tribute to Polish history. In the seventeenth century, using sweet spices in savory dishes was really popular in aristocratic courts. I would like to get back to this trend—cinnamon tastes wonderful, not just in apple pie.

MAKES	PREP TIME	COOK TIME
4 servings	15 minutes	40 minutes

8 large heirloom tomatoes (about 3 pounds/1,350 g total)

2 tablespoons (30 g) unsalted butter

1 medium white onion (5 ounces/150 g), chopped

3 garlic cloves, minced

1 teaspoon ground cinnamon

½ teaspoon cayenne pepper

¾ cup (150 g) millet

½ cup (90 g) chopped dried apricots or dried figs

½ cup (60 g) slivered almonds

1½ cups (360 ml) Vegetable Broth (page 77)

½ cup (75 g) crumbled *bryndza* or feta cheese

Extra virgin olive oil

Salt and freshly ground black pepper

1. Preheat the oven to 375°F (190°C). Slice off the tops of the tomatoes creating a 2½-inch-diameter (6.4 cm) opening at top. Set aside the tops. Using a melon baller or tablespoon, scoop out the tomato flesh, transferring the juices and pulp to a small bowl. Turn over the tomatoes, cut side down, onto paper towels to drain.

2. Heat the butter in a large skillet. Add the onion and cook, stirring occasionally, until soft and translucent, 4 to 5 minutes. Add the garlic, cinnamon, and cayenne, and cook until fragrant, about 1 minute. Stir in the millet along with the apricots, almonds, vegetable broth, and reserved tomato pulp. Cook over low heat, covered, until all the liquid has been absorbed, about 15 minutes.

3. Place the cored tomatoes upright in a baking dish and season with salt and black pepper. Stuff the tomatoes with the millet mixture and top each one with some of the cheese. Top with the saved tomato tops. Drizzle with olive oil. Bake for 20 to 25 minutes, until the tomatoes are soft. Serve hot or at room temperature.

OLIVE OIL–FRIED EGGS
with Brown Butter–Dill Potatoes and Salted Almonds

Oliwne jajka sadzone z młodym ziemniakami w palonym maśle i solonych migdałach

There is one simple summer dish that I could eat outside every day. That's new potatoes with butter and fresh dill, served with fried eggs and *Mizeria* (Creamy Cucumber Salad, page 135). Sometimes I eat them with just a glass of cold buttermilk or kefir. Browning the butter here is key—to get more nutty, earthy flavors—and those salted almonds add a delightful crunch on top of the soft potatoes. Eggs fried in hot olive oil get golden and crispy. I think I could eat these every day for a whole year.

MAKES	PREP TIME	COOK TIME
2 servings	10 minutes	20 minutes

1 pound (450 g) new potatoes or baby Yukon Gold potatoes

3 tablespoons (45 g) unsalted butter

2 tablespoons chopped fresh dill

¼ cup (40 g) salted almonds, coarsely chopped

Fine sea salt

2 tablespoons extra virgin olive oil

2 large eggs

Salt and freshly ground black pepper

1. Cook the potatoes in a large pot of boiling salted water until tender, 15 to 20 minutes. Drain the potatoes and transfer them back to the pot.

2. While the potatoes cook, make the brown butter. Heat the butter in a medium saucepan. Cook over low heat until it turns golden brown and starts smelling like nuts, 6 to 8 minutes. Remove from the heat.

3. Add the brown butter, dill, and almonds to the potatoes and carefully combine them.

4. **To make the fried eggs,** heat the olive oil in a medium skillet over medium-high heat. Crack the egg into the skillet; the oil should bubble up around the whites from the start. Season with salt and pepper. Cook until whites are golden brown, crisp at the edges, and set around the runny yolk, about 2 minutes. Immediately remove the eggs from the skillet.

5. To serve, divide the eggs and potatoes between two plates. Serve with Creamy Cucumber Salad (page 135) and a glass of cold buttermilk.

POTATO FRITTERS
with Rosemary and Horseradish Sauce
Placki ziemniaczane

This is an indulgent, beloved dish. The one that everyone will love you for because it's crispy, fried, and simply delightful. I usually eat these hot from the skillet, standing by the stove. But sometimes I put them on a beautiful plate with a super-easy horseradish and sour cream sauce, which is my refreshing complement to these little fried things.

MAKES	PREP TIME	COOK TIME
8 fritters	10 minutes	15 minutes

1 pound (450 g) starchy potatoes such as russets, peeled

1 small white onion (about 3½ ounces/100 g)

1 large egg, lightly beaten

1 teaspoon finely chopped fresh rosemary

3 tablespoons (40 g) clarified butter

½ cup (115 g) sour cream

1 teaspoon prepared white horseradish

Salt and freshly ground black pepper

1. Grate the potatoes and onion on the large holes of a box grater. Transfer to a kitchen towel, and twist tightly to wring out as much liquid as possible. Transfer the potato mixture to a bowl and stir in the egg, ¼ teaspoon salt, and the rosemary. Season with pepper.

2. Preheat the oven to 200°F (90°C). Place a wire rack on a rimmed baking sheet and set it in the oven.

3. Heat the clarified butter in a large skillet over medium-high heat until hot. Working in batches if necessary, spoon 2 tablespoons of the potato mixture per fritter into the skillet, then press gently with a fork to flatten. Reduce heat to medium and cook until undersides are browned, about 4 minutes. Turn fritters over and cook until the other sides are browned, about 4 minutes more. Transfer to paper towels to drain. Keep the fritters warm on the wire rack in the oven.

4. **To make the sauce,** mix the sour cream and horseradish in a small bowl. Season with salt and pepper. Serve the potato fritters topped with the sauce.

   Note: Starchy potatoes, grated on the large holes, make these fritters crispy (which I like), but if you want them to be more cakey and soft, use Yukon Golds and add 1 tablespoon sour cream and 1 teaspoon all-purpose flour to the batter.

BUCKWHEAT STIR-FRY
with Kale, Beans, and Goat Cheese
Smażona kasza gryczana z jarmużem, fasolą i kozim serem

As a little child I was always hungry, even after a large supper. During this tragic starvation, my grandmother would cook me buckwheat, fried in a bit of butter and served with *twaróg* in a tiny porcelain bowl. Nowadays, these grains are an ace up my sleeve after a long, tiring day, when I don't have enough energy to cook anything complicated. You can use whatever veggies are in season, but my favorite is a version with leeks, kale, beans, and spoon of soft goat cheese, which melts delightfully on the grains.

MAKES	PREP TIME	COOK TIME
2 servings	5 minutes	25 minutes

½ cup (100 g) whole buckwheat (kasha)

1 bay leaf

3 tablespoons (45 g) unsalted butter

½ leek, white and pale green parts only (about 1 ounce/25 g), halved lengthwise and thinly sliced crosswise

2 garlic cloves, minced

½ teaspoon fennel seeds

½ teaspoon dried oregano

Half a 14-ounce (400 g) can white beans, drained (about 1 cup/200 g)

3 cups (50 g) chopped kale leaves

1 teaspoon fresh lemon juice

2 tablespoons soft goat cheese

Salt and freshly ground black pepper

1. Bring 1 cup water to a boil in a small saucepan, season with salt, and add the buckwheat and bay leaf. Cook, covered, over low heat, until the grains have absorbed all the liquid, about 15 minutes. Remove from the heat and set aside, still covered.

2. Heat 2 tablespoons of the butter in a large or medium skillet. Add the leek and cook, stirring often, until it begins to soften, 4 to 5 minutes. Add the garlic, fennel seeds, oregano, and the remaining 1 tablespoon butter. Cook until fragrant, about 30 seconds. Add the beans and cooked buckwheat. Cook, stirring often, until everything is evenly coated, about 2 minutes. Add the kale and cook, tossing, until kale is tender, about 3 minutes more. Season with lemon juice, salt, and pepper.

3. To serve, divide the stir-fry between plates. Top each with 1 tablespoon of the goat cheese.

   Note: Try a version with spinach and Twaróg (page 44) instead of kale and goat cheese. You can also use about 1 cup (180 g) precooked buckwheat.

SIDE DISHES
*Sałatki, surówki
i inne dodatki*

think that the success of a meal largely depends on good side dishes. My mom won't even sit down to dinner if there isn't at least one cold salad. It's usually *Mizeria* (Creamy Cucumber Salad, page 135), *Sałatka z pomidorów z chrzanem* (Tomato Salad with Horseradish, page 148), or *Surówka z kiszonej kapusty* (Sauerkraut, Apple, and Carrot Slaw, page 132).

All these side dishes are so tempting that I even eat them solo. One of my favorites is the perfectly velvety *Sałatka z pieczonych buraków, jabłka i bundzu* (Mashed Potatoes with Cold-Pressed Rapeseed Oil, page 127). It's so good that I could eat it straight from the pot. And some of the salads from this chapter also function as a full-fledged meal, which you can proudly take with you to your friends' place. I do this often with the *Sałatka z pieczonych buraków, jabłka i bundzu* (Baked Beet, Apple and *Bundz* Salad, page 131), tossed in an addictive walnut dressing, or with the surprisingly light *Sałatka ziemniaczana z kiszonymi rzodkiewkami i gruszką* (Potato Salad with Fermented Radishes and Pear, page 128) in a French mustard sauce.

MASHED POTATOES
with Cold-Pressed Rapeseed Oil
Ziemniaczane puree z olejem rzepakowym tłoczonym na zimno

Dad, I'm sorry, but your mashed potatoes were horrible. They weren't creamy at all, with lots of chunks and peels left in. This dinnertime nightmare from my childhood inspired me to develop a simple but extraordinary version. This is a French-style purée, which normally has more butter and heavy cream than potatoes (not a bad idea at all, in my opinion!)—but my interpretation is much lighter. I switch out a ton of butter for a few tablespoons of cold-pressed rapeseed oil, which gives these potatoes a nutty scent and taste without sacrificing creaminess.

MAKES	PREP TIME	COOK TIME
4 servings	10 minutes	40 minutes

2 pounds (900 g) Yukon Gold potatoes, peeled

¼ cup heavy cream

2 garlic cloves, crushed

¼ cup (60 ml) cold-pressed rapeseed oil, plus more for serving

Salt and freshly ground black pepper

1. Place the potatoes in a large pot and cover with cold water. Add 2 tablespoons salt and bring to a boil, then reduce to a rapid simmer. Cook until the potatoes are very tender, 30 to 35 minutes. Drain, then briefly rinse the potatoes with cool water to remove any excess starch. Return to the warm pot and let dry for 1 minute.

2. While the potatoes cook, warm the cream in a small saucepan.

3. While the potatoes are still hot, mash them very carefully with the garlic. Stir in the cream and oil. Season with salt and pepper. Serve with another drizzle of oil.

   Note: These mashed potatoes can be made up to 2 days ahead. Store them covered in the fridge. You can reheat them on the stovetop over medium heat, adding a bit of milk or vegetable stock to loosen the consistency. You can also fry them in a pan with melted butter, which gives them a nice crunch.

POTATO SALAD
with Fermented Radishes and Pear
Sałatka ziemniaczana z kiszonymi rzodkiewkami i gruszką

Potato salad is considered a German-style dish, heavy in mayonnaise, sour cream, and onion. In my opinion, all that is too heavy for a "salad." I prefer to swap out the mayo and cream for a sweet-tangy whole grain mustard dressing and crunchy pickled radishes. My homemade radishes have a punch of allspice, which works here perfectly with the sweetness of pears. It isn't odd—it's extraordinarily good.

	MAKES	PREP TIME	COOK TIME
	6 servings	10 minutes	15 minutes

2 pounds (900 g) waxy potatoes, scrubbed and halved

2 tablespoons honey

2 tablespoons fresh lemon juice

3 tablespoons whole grain mustard

¼ cup (60 ml) cold-pressed rapeseed oil

2 medium (450 g) pears, cored and chopped

1½ cups (210 g) Salt-Brined Fermented Radishes (page 235), chopped

½ cup (15 g) coarsely chopped fresh parsley, plus more for serving

Salt and freshly ground black pepper

1. Place the potatoes in a large pot and pour in cold water to cover. Season generously with salt. Bring to a boil, then reduce the heat and simmer until tender, about 15 minutes. Drain and return them to the pot to dry out. Let cool only slightly—the potatoes should be warm when you dress them, which will help them soak up the flavors.

2. While the potatoes cook, make the dressing. Mix the honey and lemon juice in a small jar. Add the mustard and oil, seal the jar, and shake vigorously until dressing is smooth, about 10 seconds. Season with salt and pepper.

3. Toss the cooked potatoes, pears, radishes, and parsley with the dressing in a medium bowl. Season with pepper. Divide onto plates, and top with additional parsley.

Note: This salad is really good with fermented radishes, but you can also use Ogórki kiszone (Salt-Brined Dill Pickles, page 231) in a pinch.

BAKED BEET, APPLE, AND *BUNDZ* SALAD

Sałatka z pieczonych buraków, jabłka i bundzu

This salad is a good example of the magic that can occur when you treat every crucial ingredient very differently—in this case, raw and roasted. Beets are roasted while wrapped in aluminum foil, which helps condense the flavor and make them pleasantly soft. The tender beets mingle with chopped juicy apple, which turns a lovely pink from touching the beets. The walnut dressing pairs perfectly with this earthy combination. A cold glass of apple cider is a delightful accompaniment to this salad.

MAKES	PREP TIME	COOK TIME
4 servings	15 minutes	1½ hours

6 medium beets (about 600 g), scrubbed, leaves and stems removed

2 tablespoons sunflower oil

3 large Granny Smith apples (about 1½ pounds/600 g total)

1 bunch parsley (about 1 cup/ 30 g), plus more for serving

¼ cup (40 g) walnuts, chopped

⅔ cup (70 g) crumbled *bundz* or feta cheese

FOR THE WALNUT DRESSING

¾ cup (120 g) walnuts

1 garlic clove

½ cup (90 ml) cold-pressed rapeseed oil

¼ cup (60 ml) fresh lemon juice (about 2 lemons)

1 tablespoon honey

Salt and freshly ground black pepper

1. Preheat the oven to 375°F (190°C). Coat the beets lightly with oil and wrap them individually in aluminum foil. Place the foil packets on a baking sheet, and roast for 1 to 1½ hours, until cooked through and fork-tender.

2. Remove the beets from the oven and open the foil packets to release the heat. Let cool for 10 minutes, or until cool enough to handle. Peel the beets and chop them into ¼-inch (6 mm) cubes.

3. Peel and chop the apples into 1-inch (2.5 cm) cubes. Finely chop the parsley. Set everything aside.

4. **To make the dressing,** toast the walnuts in a heated skillet on the stove, tossing occasionally, until golden brown, 8 to 10 minutes. Let them cool, then finely chop.

5. Combine ½ cup of the toasted walnuts, garlic, and oil in a food processor and blend to a coarse purée. Stir in the remaining ¼ cup toasted walnuts, the lemon juice, and honey. Season with salt and pepper.

6. **To assemble the salad,** toss the beets, apples, and parsley in a large bowl with half of the dressing, then drizzle the remaining dressing over the top. Divide among plates and top with the walnuts, cheese, and additional parsley.

SAUERKRAUT, APPLE, AND CARROT SLAW

Surówka z kiszonej kapusty

The word *surówka* refers to a slaw with two important qualities: the vegetables must be raw or pickled, and it should "bite together." In other words, a *surówka* tends to taste better over time. This sauerkraut one is one of the most popular Polish dishes, but every household has its own version—with or without apple and onion, seasoned with caraway seeds or not, and so on. This is my dad's favorite recipe, but the splash of cold-pressed rapeseed oil and drizzle of honey are my personal touches.

MAKES	PREP TIME
4 servings	5 minutes

10½ ounces (2 cups/300 g) Sauerkraut (page 232)

2 medium Gala apples (about 12 ounces/350 g total), cored and grated

1 medium carrot (about 2½ ounces/70 g), peeled and grated

2 tablespoons cold-pressed rapeseed oil or extra virgin olive oil

1 teaspoon honey

1 teaspoon caraway seeds, ground

Salt and freshly ground black pepper

1. Place the sauerkraut in a colander and squeeze out all excess liquid using your hands. Chop well.

2. Combine the sauerkraut, apples, and carrot in a large bowl. Add the oil and honey, and toss to combine. Season with the caraway and salt and pepper.

CREAMY CUCUMBER SALAD
Mizeria

When the summer season starts, I can never decide if I prefer juicy, sweet tomatoes or refreshing cucumbers eaten with a few sea salt flakes. At least I know one thing: in a salad with sour cream, cucumbers taste marvelous. Light and creamy, this salad has lots of fresh dill and shallot, which adds a nice bite.

MAKES	PREP TIME
2 to 4 servings	15 minutes

2 medium (14 ounces/400 g) English cucumbers, peeled

2 tablespoons sour cream

2 tablespoons chopped fresh dill, plus more for serving

1 small shallot, thinly sliced

Salt and freshly ground black pepper

1. Slice the cucumbers very thinly. Transfer them to a medium bowl, add ½ teaspoon salt, and massage the cucumbers with your fingers. Allow the salt to draw out the water from the cucumbers.

2. Rinse the cucumbers well with water to remove excess salt, then drain. Return them to the bowl, add the sour cream, dill, and shallot, and stir to combine. Season with salt and pepper. Top with extra dill and serve immediately.

CREAMY HOT BEETS

Buraczki na ciepło

There are some things that bring me into a blissful oblivion—and these hot beets are one of them. I don't know if it's their sweetness, balanced with sour cream and a bit of lemon, or maybe it's the creaminess and warmth that goes so well with mashed potatoes. It's one of those simple dishes that my grandmother used to make that tastes absolutely the best for me.

MAKES	PREP TIME	COOK TIME
4 servings	5 minutes	10 minutes

6 small beets (1 pound/ 450 g)

1 tablespoon all-purpose flour

1 tablespoon (15 g) unsalted butter

2 tablespoons sour cream

½ teaspoon honey

1 teaspoon fresh lemon juice

Salt and freshly ground black pepper

1. Put the beets in a large pot of salted water and bring to a boil. Cook until the beets are soft, about 40 minutes. Drain the beets and let them cool slightly.

2. Peel and finely grate the cooked beets. Combine them with the flour, butter, sour cream, honey, and ¼ teaspoon salt in a medium saucepan. Cook over medium heat, stirring frequently, until the mixture boils and thickens, about 5 minutes.

3. Stir in the lemon juice. Season with pepper to taste, and more salt if needed. Serve immediately.

Note: *These beets can be reheated the next day in a saucepan with small amount of water.*

SAUTÉED CUCUMBERS
with Fennel Seeds

Podsmażane ogórki z nasionami kopru włoskiego

The destiny of the cucumber has changed over the centuries. Now we eat them raw, often with sour cream such as in *Mizeria* (Creamy Cucumber Salad, page 135), on sandwiches, or in salads. But they can be stuffed, braised in sour cream, or even served with thick, rich sauces. In seventeenth-century *staropolska* (Old Polish) cuisine, cucumbers were used as a base for soups or as hot appetizers. There are many options worth considering, because warm cucumbers are really delicious. My favorite way to eat them is sautéed with a bit of butter and fresh fennel seeds.

MAKES	PREP TIME	RESTING TIME	COOK TIME
2 or 3 servings	5 minutes	30 minutes	5 minutes

2 medium cucumbers
  (1 pound/450 g total)

½ teaspoon salt

1 tablespoon (15 g) unsalted
  butter

1 garlic clove, chopped

1 teaspoon fennel seeds, ground

1 teaspoon apple cider vinegar

Chopped fresh dill

1. Cut the cucumbers in half lengthwise and scoop out the pulp and seeds with a teaspoon. Cut each half again lengthwise. Place the cucumbers in a bowl and sprinkle with the salt; mix well and set aside for at least 30 minutes.

2. Rinse the cucumbers to remove excess salt, then drain. Heat the butter in a medium skillet over medium heat. Add the garlic and fennel seeds; cook until fragrant, 30 to 60 seconds. Add the cucumbers; cook to heat them and drive in the flavors. Remove from the heat.

3. To serve, transfer them to a serving dish and top with dill.

BUTTERY PEAS
with Salted Almonds and Parsley
Maślany groszek z solonymi migdałami i pietruszką

This dish is best enjoyed in those fleeting weeks of spring when sweet garden peas are in season and easily available in farmers markets. The particularly delicate combination with salty, crunchy almonds relies on the sweetness of spring peas and a bit of butter to enhance the flavor. If you can't find fresh garden peas, you can substitute frozen peas, but make sure to add a good amount of honey to bring out this dish's lovely sweetness.

MAKES	COOK TIME
4 to 6 servings	10 minutes

1 pound (450 g) shelled peas, fresh or frozen and thawed

2 tablespoons (30 g) unsalted butter

1 teaspoon fresh lemon juice

½ teaspoon honey

½ cup (80 g) salted roasted almonds, chopped

2 tablespoons chopped fresh parsley

Salt and freshly ground black pepper

1. In a large pot of water over medium heat, cook the peas until soft, 5 to 8 minutes (less if using frozen). Remove from the heat. Drain, and return to the pot.

2. Stir in the butter, lemon juice, and honey. Add the almonds and parsley. Season with salt and pepper. Serve immediately.

FAVA BEANS
with Mint and Garlic
Bób z miętą i czosnkiem

In summer in Poland, you will find fava beans, already shelled, packed in a bag, for sale at every market. The most popular way to prepare them is simply by cooking them in a big pot of salted water and serving them in their skins, without any additions, as a summer snack. There is something about the way the kitchen fills with the scent of beans on hot days, and about the softness of beans that slip out of their skins in your hands. When fava beans are young and fresh, they can be eaten raw, even with their thin skin. I like them blanched and sautéed with a bit of butter and olive oil, which coat the beans with a delicious, salty sauce. At the end, I toss in a bunch of fresh mint.

MAKES	COOK TIME
2 to 4 servings	15 minutes

1 pound (2½ cups/450 g) shelled fresh fava beans or thawed frozen fava beans

1 tablespoon (15 g) unsalted butter

1 tablespoon extra virgin olive oil

3 garlic cloves, minced

1 cup (30 g) loosely packed fresh mint leaves

Salt and freshly ground black pepper

1. Bring a large pot of salted water to a boil and set a colander in a large bowl filled with ice and water. Add the fava beans to the boiling water and cook until just tender, about 5 minutes. Reserve ¼ cup (60 ml) of the cooking water. Using a mesh sieve, transfer the favas to the colander; let sit briefly until cool. Drain. Remove the skins, if desired.

2. Heat the butter and the olive oil in the saucepan. Cook the garlic 30 seconds, until fragrant. Add the fava beans and cook, stirring gently, until they are coated in the fat. Stir in the reserved cooking water and cook until the sauce becomes thick. Remove from the heat. Toss in the mint and season with salt and pepper. Serve immediately.

BRAISED CABBAGE
with Hazelnuts
Modra kapusta

Polish cuisine in the sixteenth century was rich in Asian spices, which were used generously, even in main dishes. My version of *modra kapusta* is a small tribute to those old flavors of Poland. This braised cabbage is slightly sweet and aromatic, with a crunchiness from the hazelnuts. Usually, I serve it as side dish, but it will also taste great with a buttered slice of bread and a piece of blue cheese.

MAKES	PREP TIME	COOK TIME
6 servings	10 minutes	45 minutes

½ cup (75 g) raw skin-on hazelnuts

1 teaspoon fennel seeds

1 teaspoon cumin seeds

2 tablespoons (30 g) unsalted butter

½ teaspoon ground cinnamon

1 small head red cabbage (about 2 pounds/900 g), cored and thinly sliced

3 tablespoons soy sauce

1 tart apple (about 6 ounces/180 g), such as Granny Smith, peeled and grated

2 tablespoons apple cider vinegar

1 tablespoon honey

Salt and freshly ground black pepper

1. Preheat the oven to 350°F (180°C). Toast the hazelnuts on a rimmed baking sheet, tossing once, until fragrant and slightly darkened, about 10 minutes. Cool completely. Using a kitchen towel, rub the hazelnuts together to remove most of the skins. (Don't worry about some stubborn bits remaining.) Chop the nuts roughly.

2. Grind the fennel and cumin seeds with a mortar and pestle or in a spice grinder.

3. Heat the butter in a large skillet over medium heat. Add the ground spices and cinnamon; cook until fragrant, 1 to 2 minutes. Add the cabbage, 1 cup water, and 2 tablespoons of the soy sauce. Cook, covered, over low heat, until cabbage is tender, 20 to 30 minutes. Add the hazelnuts, apples, vinegar, honey, and the remaining tablespoon soy sauce. Season with salt and pepper. Serve hot.

SPRING MILLET SALAD

Sałatka z kaszy jaglanej, rzodkiewek, szparagów i szpinaku

Asparagus is my favorite, because it's the first vegetable to appear after the long, cold winter, and you can only enjoy it for a few weeks of the year. Green and crunchy, it tastes best quickly cooked in boiling water and served simply with a little butter and salt. This fresh, spring salad is excellent way to use asparagus. The base is hearty millet, with handfuls of spinach and pink radishes. It's perfect as a side dish, or as a main with a bit of feta cheese sprinkled on top.

MAKES	PREP TIME	COOK TIME
4 to 6 servings	10 minutes	15 minutes

1 cup (200 g) millet

1 bunch (1 pound/450 g) green asparagus, trimmed

10 radishes (5 ounces/150 g total), trimmed and sliced

1 small red onion (4 ounces/ 120 g), chopped

2 loosely packed cups (60 g) baby spinach

3 tablespoons cold-pressed rapeseed oil, plus more for serving

1 teaspoon fresh lemon juice

Fresh mint (optional)

Salt and freshly ground black pepper

1. Bring 2 cups salted water to a boil in a medium saucepan. Stir in the millet; cook, covered, over low heat until all liquid has been absorbed, 15 minutes. Remove from the heat.

2. Fill a large bowl with ice and water. Bring a medium pot of water to a boil, then add the asparagus and cook until bright green and tender, about 3 minutes. Using a slotted spoon, transfer the asparagus to the ice water to cool; drain, then pat dry with paper towels.

3. Place the millet, asparagus, radishes, onion, and spinach in a large bowl, sprinkle with the oil and lemon juice, and stir to combine. Season with salt and pepper. Drizzle with more oil, top with mint leaves, if desired, and serve.

TOMATO SALAD
with Horseradish
Sałatka z pomidorów z chrzanem

Sweet, juicy summer tomatoes from the farmers market are incomparable. I eat them alone or with just a pinch of flaky sea salt. But this horseradish dressing has an earthy, sharp taste, which complements them so well and makes them taste even better.

MAKES	PREP TIME
2 servings	5 minutes

1½ tablespoons prepared white horseradish

2 tablespoons cold-pressed rapeseed oil

1 teaspoon fresh lemon juice

1 teaspoon honey

12 ounces (340 g) tomatoes, preferably cherry tomatoes, halved

2 tablespoons chopped fresh parsley, plus more for serving

Flaky sea salt

Salt and freshly ground black pepper

1. Stir together the horseradish, rapeseed oil, lemon juice, and honey in a medium bowl. Season with salt and pepper.

2. Add the tomatoes and parsley; coat carefully with the dressing. Top with more pepper, flaky sea salt, and more parsley.

   Note: *Try a version with 1 or 2 tablespoons of slivered almonds, which tastes even better.*

PIEROGI AND DUMPLINGS

Pierogi i inne kluski

Making pierogi is so relaxing. It's a moment when you can sit down, gather your thoughts, and don't have to rush anywhere. My favorite way is to make them with my family or friends. I invite them over, usually on Sunday when everybody has free time, we open some beer or cider, and have a pierogi party. There are always several different fillings. Firstly, *Pierogi Ruskie* (page 157) with potatoes, caramelized onion, and *twaróg*. They are probably the most popular pierogi in Poland. My second favorite is *Pierogi z kiszoną kapustą, grzybami i kandyzowaną skórką z pomarańczy* (Pierogi with Sauerkraut, Mushrooms, and Candied Orange Zest, page 158), typically served on Christmas Eve, but I can't resist eating them more than once a year. You can fill your pierogi with anything, cooking various vegetables, beans, and dairy, and then stuffing the dumplings of your dreams.

In my family, one filling is especially important—sour cherries. It's our July tradition. My uncle picks the fruit from the tree, which has grown in our yard for fifty years, my grandmother kneads the dough, and I stuff the pierogi with exactly three cherries per piece. We serve them with the whipped vanilla sour cream from the *Pierogi z jagodami i miodową kwaśną śmietaną* (Blueberry Pierogi with Honeyed Sour Cream, page 169). And we eat way too many every year.

BASIC PIEROGI DOUGH

Ciasto na pierogi

Everyone thinks that their recipe for dumpling dough is the best. I do, too. Many pierogi recipes contain yolks or whole eggs. But I don't use them, because I think they make the dough harder. My key to success is a large amount of cold-pressed rapeseed oil, which makes the dough perfectly soft and gives it an amazing nutty scent. The consistency is the most important part—sometimes you have to sprinkle the dough with more flour or add a little water to achieve a nice ball. Practice makes perfect: Keep trying, and soon you will be just like a real Polish grandmother.

MAKES	PREP TIME	RESTING TIME	COOK TIME
50 pierogi, 4 to 6 servings	30 minutes	15 minutes	10 minutes

3½ cups (450 g) all-purpose flour, plus more for kneading and holding

1 teaspoon salt

¼ cup (60 ml) cold-pressed rapeseed oil or extra virgin olive oil

1 tablespoon sunflower oil

1. Combine the flour and salt in a large bowl. In a separate bowl, combine the rapeseed oil and 1 cup (230 ml) warm water. Slowly add the liquid ingredients to the flour and mix with a wooden spoon until the dough is well combined. Turn the dough out onto a clean, lightly floured surface and knead for 4 to 5 minutes, until it is smooth and supple. Invert a bowl over the dough and let it rest at room temperature for at least 15 minutes to allow the gluten to relax.

2. Divide the dough into three equal pieces. Place one piece on a lightly floured surface. (Cover the remaining dough with a clean kitchen towel to keep it from drying out.) Using a rolling pin, roll out the dough to a thickness of just less than ⅛ inch (3 mm), lifting up the dough to dust the surface with flour to prevent sticking, if needed.

3. Using a pastry cutter or inverted glass tumbler, cut out 2½-inch (6.4 cm) diameter circles of dough. Roll out the circles even thinner, to 3 inches (7.6 cm). Gather the dough scraps into a ball and set aside. Continue with the other two pieces of dough, and the combined scraps, until all dough is used, making 30 to 50 circles.

4. Put 1 to 2 tablespoons filling in the center of each round, leaving a ¾-inch (2 cm) border. Grasp the dough from opposite ends and pull it up and over the filling, pressing down to seal the edges together and creating a semicircle. Pinch the edges together to seal completely. If the edges don't adhere, brush them lightly with water, then seal. Do not leave any gaps or the pierogi may open during cooking.

5. Transfer the pierogi to a lightly floured kitchen towel and cover with another towel to prevent drying. Continue until all the dough is used.

6. Boil a large pot of salted water and add the sunflower oil. Working in batches, use a slotted spoon to gently lower 10 to 15 pierogi at a time into the pot. When the pierogi rise to the surface, continue to cook them for 1 to 2 minutes more, then transfer with the spoon to a colander to drain immediately. Serve with butter and sour cream.

Note: Uncooked pierogi can be stored for up to 2 months. Freeze on baking sheets for about 1 hour, then transfer to a resealable plastic bag. Boil them straight from the freezer, adding 2 minutes to the overall cooking time.

PIEROGI RUSKIE

One of the most beloved Polish classics, *pierogi ruskie* ("Russian" pierogi), actually have nothing to do with Russia. These pierogi are filled with potatoes mashed with *twaróg* and a bit of golden-brown onion. The farmer cheese should be fatty and the best quality you can find. It's also important to add a huge amount of freshly ground black pepper, enough so that it pinches your tongue. Pierogi taste excellent when they are fried, and also straight from the cooking water. In that case, I recommend serving them with warm nutty brown butter. My great-grandmother did it that way, and she really knew her stuff.

MAKES	PREP TIME	COOK TIME
about 50 pierogi, 4 to 6 servings	40 minutes	20 minutes

3 starchy potatoes, such as russets (about 1 pound/500 g total), peeled and chopped

12 ounces (2 cups/340 g) farmer cheese or *Twaróg* (page 44)

2 tablespoons (30 g) unsalted butter

3 small white onions (10 ounces/ 300 g total), chopped

Basic Pierogi Dough (page 154)

¼ cup (½ stick/60 g) unsalted butter

Fresh thyme

Sour cream

Flaky sea salt, for serving

Salt and freshly ground black pepper

1. Boil the potatoes in generously salted water. Cook until soft, 15 to 20 minutes. Drain, then return them to the pot. Mash the potatoes, add the cheese, and mash again.

2. While the potatoes are boiling, heat the butter in a large skillet. Add the onion and cook, stirring frequently, until golden brown, 10 to 15 minutes. Add the onion to the potato-cheese mixture with ½ teaspoon pepper, and stir to combine. Season with salt and more pepper, to taste. (The filling should be very peppery.) Let cool completely.

3. Meanwhile, make the pierogi dough. Following the instructions, fill, cook, and drain the pierogi.

4. Heat the butter in a medium saucepan. Cook over low heat until it turns golden brown and starts smelling like nuts, 6 to 8 minutes. Remove from the heat.

5. To serve, divide the pierogi among plates. Drizzle with the brown butter, top with thyme, and serve with sour cream.

PIEROGI
with Sauerkraut, Mushrooms, and Candied Orange Zest

Pierogi z kiszoną kapustą, grzybami i kandyzowaną skórką z pomarańczy

These pierogi are usually served as part of a traditional Polish Christmas Eve dinner—a feast of twelve dishes—but I like them so much that I cook them all year long. Sauerkraut filling may be too acidic for some, so I tone it down with candied orange zest, which gives these a delicate sweetness and a Christmas-y relish.

MAKES	PREP TIME	COOK TIME
about 30 pierogi, 4 servings	30 minutes	1 hour

1 pound (3 cups/450 g) Sauerkraut (page 232), drained and finely chopped

¼ cup plus 3 tablespoons (105 g) unsalted butter

1 medium onion (6 ounces/180 g), chopped

2 bay leaves

1 pound (450 g) oyster mushrooms (see Note), chopped

1 small carrot (about 3½ ounces/100 g), peeled and grated

5 tablespoons (90 g) chopped candied orange zest

Basic Pierogi Dough (page 154)

1 whole star anise pod

2 whole cloves

Salt and freshly ground black pepper

1. **To make the filling,** place the sauerkraut in a medium saucepan and cover with water. Cook over low heat for 40 minutes, until tender. Drain well.

2. Heat 1 tablespoon of the butter in a large skillet. Add the onion and the bay leaves. Cook, stirring occasionally, until the onion is translucent, 3 to 4 minutes. Add another tablespoon of butter, let it melt, then add the mushrooms. Cook for 5 to 8 minutes, until golden brown. Add another tablespoon of butter, then the sauerkraut, carrot, and 2 tablespoons of the candied orange zest. Cook for 2 minutes more, until flavors combine. Discard the bay leaves, then season with salt and pepper. Let cool completely.

3. Meanwhile, make the pierogi dough. Following the instructions, fill, cook, and drain the pierogi.

4. **To make the topping,** heat the remaining 4 tablespoons (60 g) butter, 3 tablespoons candied orange zest, and the star anise and cloves in a small saucepan. Remove from heat to let the flavors develop.

5. To serve, divide the pierogi among plates and spoon a generous amount of the topping over them.

    Note: You can also use 4 ounces (115 g) dried mushrooms, cooked for 40 minutes, instead of the oyster mushrooms.

PIEROGI
with Buckwheat, *Bryndza,* and Mint
Pierogi z kaszą gryczaną, bryndzą i miętą

This is my grandma's favorite pierogi. She used to make them twice the size of normal pierogi, but it's also possible that I was very little and just remember them like that. I would ask her for three, but four or five giant pierogi always appeared on my plate. She was very generous with her pierogi, filling them with nutty buckwheat and *twaróg* cheese. My version uses sheep's milk *bryndza,* a regional product of the Podhale region. If you don't have a good Polish deli nearby, you can substitute feta cheese. I also like adding mint for an incredibly refreshing punch.

MAKES	PREP TIME	COOK TIME
about 30 pierogi, 4 servings	40 minutes, plus chilling	20 minutes

1 cup (150 g) whole buckwheat (kasha)

1 tablespoon (15 g) unsalted butter

1 medium white onion (6 ounces/180 g), chopped

1 cup fresh mint leaves, finely chopped, plus more for serving

1 cup (150 g) *bryndza* or feta cheese, crumbled

Basic Pierogi Dough (page 154)

Cold-pressed rapeseed oil

Sour cream

Salt and freshly ground pepper

1. **To make the filling,** boil 2 cups salted water in a medium saucepan. Add the buckwheat and cook, covered, over low heat for 15 minutes, until all the liquid has been absorbed. Remove from the heat and keep covered.

2. While the buckwheat cooks, heat the butter in a large skillet over medium heat. Add the onion and cook, stirring occasionally, until translucent, 3 to 4 minutes. Add the cooked buckwheat, mint, and cheese. Cook, stirring occasionally, for 2 to 3 minutes, until well-combined. Season with salt if needed (the cheese is already very salty) and pepper. Let cool completely.

3. Meanwhile, make the pierogi dough. Following the instructions, fill, cook, and drain the pierogi.

4. To serve, divide the pierogi among plates. Top with more mint, a drizzle of cold-pressed rapeseed oil, and a dollop of sour cream.

PIEROGI
with Spinach, Goat Cheese, and Salted Almonds

Pierogi ze szpinakiem, serem kozim i solonymi migdałami

Spinach often brings back traumatic memories from childhood—in my case, I can't shake the thought of the green mass with a strange consistency that was served every Thursday at school. But spinach takes on a new, amazing flavor in these pierogi. The filling is enriched with goat cheese that melts in the mouth, as well as crunchy, salted almonds and a little lemon zest for freshness. To serve, I sprinkle Parmesan over them for an Italian twist. Delicious!

MAKES	PREP TIME	COOK TIME
about 30 pierogi, 2 or 3 servings	30 minutes, plus chilling	10 minutes

2 tablespoons (30 g) unsalted butter

1 medium red onion (about 5 ounces/150 g), chopped

3 garlic cloves, chopped

7 ounces (200 g) fresh spinach

¼ cup (7 g) chopped fresh parsley

¼ cup (30 g) chopped salted almonds

½ teaspoon grated lemon zest

½ cup (100 g) soft goat cheese

½ recipe Basic Pierogi Dough (page 154)

Cold-pressed rapeseed oil

Grated Parmesan cheese

Salt and freshly ground black pepper

1. **To make the filling,** heat the butter in a large skillet over medium-low heat. Add the onion and cook, stirring occasionally, until translucent, 3 to 4 minutes. Add the garlic and cook, stirring constantly, until fragrant, about 30 seconds. Add the spinach, season with salt and pepper, and cook, tossing, until it starts to wilt. Remove from the heat and let cool.

2. Transfer the spinach mixture to a cutting board and roughly chop it. Transfer it to a medium bowl. Add the parsley, almonds, lemon zest, and cheese and stir to combine.

3. Meanwhile, make the pierogi dough. Following the instructions, fill, cook, and drain the pierogi.

4. To serve, divide the pierogi among plates. Top with cold-pressed rapeseed oil and Parmesan cheese.

PIEROGI
with Lentils and Dried Tomatoes
Pierogi z soczewicą i suszonymi pomidorami

Cumin and coriander were popular spices in the Polish cuisine of the seventeenth century. Nowadays, they are making a comeback thanks to the hummus trend. I'm happy about it, because I can mix these spices with lentils to make a wonderful pierogi filling. My favorite version is a fried one—the different textures here are comforting: crispy dough and soft spiced lentils.

MAKES	PREP TIME	COOK TIME
about 30 pierogi, 2 or 3 servings	30 minutes, plus chilling	50 minutes

¾ cup (150 g) green lentils

2 bay leaves

2 tablespoons (30 g) unsalted butter

1 medium white onion (6 ounces/180 g), chopped

3 garlic cloves, thinly sliced

¾ teaspoon coriander seeds, ground

½ teaspoon cumin seeds, ground

½ cup (50 g) sun-dried tomatoes, chopped

1 tablespoon soy sauce

½ recipe Basic Pierogi Dough (page 154)

3 tablespoons (40 g) clarified butter

Grated Parmesan cheese

Salt and freshly ground black pepper

1. Cook the lentils with the bay leaves in a large pot of water, until soft, 30 to 40 minutes. When the lentils are almost cooked, season with salt. (Cooking lentils in salted water will make them hard.) Drain the lentils and discard the bay leaves.

2. Heat the butter in a medium skillet over medium heat. Add the onion and cook until soft, 4 to 5 minutes. Add the garlic, coriander, and cumin and cook until fragrant, about 1 minute. Add the sun-dried tomatoes and soy sauce and stir to combine. Remove from the heat. Season with salt and pepper. Chill completely.

3. Meanwhile, make the pierogi dough. Following the instructions, fill, cook, and drain the pierogi.

4. Heat 1 tablespoon clarified butter in a medium skillet over medium heat. Add a few cooked pierogi; cook, turning once, until golden brown and crisp on both sides, about 3 minutes total. Transfer to a plate and top with Parmesan. Repeat with remaining pierogi, adding more clarified butter to the pan if needed.

POTATO *KNEDLE*
with Plums and Cinnamon-Honey Butter
Knedle ze śliwkami i masłem cunamonowo-miodowym

During plum season, everybody freaks out about these. These dumplings, made from a potato dough wrapped around a whole ripe fruit, are one of the biggest treasures of autumn in Poland. I stuff them with cinnamon-honey butter as well. When you break through the dumpling skin, topped with crispy caramelized bread crumbs, the cinnamon-honey butter bursts through, together with the plum juices.

MAKES	PREP TIME	CHILLING TIME	COOK TIME
20 to 30 dumplings, 4 servings	30 minutes	20 minutes	30 minutes

FOR THE PLUM FILLING

¼ cup (½ stick/60 g) unsalted butter, at room temperature

3 tablespoons honey

1 teaspoon ground cinnamon

12 ounces (340 g) ripe Italian or damson plums (20 to 30 plums)

FOR THE DOUGH

1 pound (450 g) russet potatoes, peeled and chopped

Salt

1 large egg, lightly beaten

1 cup (130 g) all-purpose flour, plus more as needed

1 tablespoon cornstarch

FOR THE TOPPING

3 tablespoons (45 g) unsalted butter

2 tablespoons bread crumbs

Pinch of sugar

Pinch of salt

1. **To make the filling,** combine the butter, honey, and cinnamon. Cut the plums lengthwise along the seam on one side (do not cut them completely in half) and take out the pits. Fill each plum with about ½ teaspoon of the cinnamon-honey butter. Chill the plums in the refrigerator until the butter sets, at least 20 minutes.

2. Cook the potatoes in a large pot of salted water until soft, about 20 minutes. Drain, then return them to the pot. Mash them, then transfer to a medium bowl and let cool completely.

3. Add the egg, flour, cornstarch, and ¼ teaspoon salt to the mashed potatoes and stir to combine. Knead the mixture with your hands until a soft dough forms that no longer sticks to your hands. Add more flour as needed.

4. Turn out the dough onto a floured surface. Cut the dough into equal pieces, depending on the number of plums. (The dough should be about twice the size of a plum.) With floured hands, pat each piece of dough flat, big enough to completely cover a plum. Place a filled plum on each one, fold the dough over, and pinch all the way around to seal.

5. Bring a large pot of lightly salted water to a boil and place all of the dumplings in it. When the dumplings float to the top, cook for an additional 5 minutes.

6. While the dumplings cook, make the topping. Heat the butter in a large skillet over medium heat. Add the bread crumbs, sugar, and salt and cook, stirring occasionally, for a few minutes, until golden brown.

7. Drain the dumplings well, then transfer them to the skillet. Cook for 1 to 2 minutes, turning them occasionally, until they are golden and coated with the bread crumbs. Serve warm.

Note: You'll definitely have leftover cinnamon-honey butter—it tastes divine spread on toasted Sourdough Rye Bread (page 64) or Whole Wheat Challah (page 55).

BLUEBERRY PIEROGI
with Honeyed Sour Cream
Pierogi z jagodami i miodową kwaśną śmietaną

Polish summer feels like hot days, strong sunlight, and walks to the farmers market for jars of wild blueberries. Then lazily making pierogi, stuffing them with as many blueberries as possible, trying not to stain your fingers with the sweet purple juice flowing out of them. I like adding a bit of cardamom to the blueberry filling, to give it a bit of fairytale flavor. Served straight from the cooking water, with sour cream and honey, these are the best summer treat.

MAKES	PREP TIME	COOK TIME
about 40 pierogi, 4 servings	30 minutes	15 minutes

1 pound (450 g) blueberries, fresh or thawed frozen, plus more for serving

1 tablespoon cornstarch

4 tablespoons honey, plus more for serving

¾ teaspoon ground cardamom

Basic Pierogi Dough (page 154)

1 cup (240 g) sour cream or crème fraîche

1 teaspoon pure vanilla extract

1. **To make the filling,** combine the blueberries, cornstarch, 3 tablespoons of the honey, and the cardamom in a large bowl.

2. Make the pierogi dough. Following the instructions, fill, cook, and drain the pierogi.

3. While the pierogi are cooking, beat the sour cream, vanilla, and the remaining 1 tablespoon honey together until slightly fluffy, about 5 minutes.

4. To serve, divide the pierogi among plates and top with the sour cream, additional blueberries, and honey.

   Note: In the summer, the Polish countryside is studded with jagody, *also known as wild blueberries or bilberries. For a taste of Poland, use bilberries instead of blueberries, if you can find them!*

PIEROGI
with Prunes, Orange, and Walnuts
Pierogi z suszonymi śliwkami, skórką pomarańczową i orzechami włoskimi

To be honest, pierogi with prunes weren't my favorite growing up. My grandma used to make these every Christmas Eve, mostly to spoil my uncle, who can easily eat a dozen of them. She puts a beautiful whole dried plum in a piece of dough and cooks it, but I prefer to blend the prunes to a smooth paste flavored with orange and cinnamon. Chopped walnuts add a pleasant contrast to these soft dumplings.

MAKES	PREP TIME	COOK TIME
about 20 pierogi, 2 to 4 servings	30 minutes	10 minutes

1¼ cups (200 g) prunes, pitted and chopped

2 tablespoons grated orange zest

¼ cup plus 2 tablespoons (45 g) chopped walnuts

Pinch of salt

½ recipe Basic Pierogi Dough (page 154)

⅓ cup (50 g) bread crumbs

3 tablespoons (45 g) unsalted butter

¼ cup (60 ml) sour cream

Ground cinnamon

1. **To make the filling,** soak the prunes in hot water until soft, about 30 minutes, then drain. Transfer the prunes to a blender and blend to a smooth paste. Stir in the orange zest, ¼ cup (30 g) of the walnuts, and the salt.

2. Make the pierogi dough. Following the instructions, fill, cook, and drain the pierogi.

3. While the pierogi cook, make the fried bread crumbs. Heat a medium skillet over medium heat. Add the bread crumbs and the remaining 2 tablespoons walnuts and toss until golden, about 2 minutes. Add the butter and cinnamon and cook, stirring, until golden brown, about 2 minutes.

4. To serve, divide the pierogi among plates. Top with the fried bread crumbs and serve with sour cream and a pinch of cinnamon.

USZKA DUMPLINGS WITH PORCINI
Uszka z borowikami

Charmingly small and generously filled with dainty wild forest porcini, these are among my most beloved dumplings. Traditionally, on Christmas Eve, *uszka* ("little ears") float in *Barszcz czysty czerwony* (Clear Fermented Beet Soup, page 78), which gives them a lovely color and even more flavor. They are perfect when they're fresh, but save some to reheat—served with butter and chives, and eaten while sitting on the couch, they're a perfect little treat for after your holiday guests have left.

MAKES	PREP TIME	COOK TIME
about 25 dumplings, 4 servings	30 minutes	15 minutes

1 ounce (30 g) dried mushrooms, preferably porcini

2 tablespoons (30 g) unsalted butter

1 medium onion (6 ounces/180 g), finely chopped

1 tablespoon soy sauce

1 tablespoon bread crumbs

½ recipe Basic Pierogi Dough (page 154)

1 tablespoon sunflower oil

Salt and freshly ground black pepper

1. Cover the dried mushrooms with about 1 cup water in a medium saucepan. Bring to a boil. Reduce the heat to low and cook until soft, about 30 minutes.

2. Drain the mushrooms; save the liquid for another purpose (see Note). Chop the mushrooms very finely and set aside.

3. Heat 1 tablespoon (15 g) of the butter in a medium skillet over medium heat. Add the onion and a pinch of salt; cook until soft, 5 to 6 minutes. Add the remaining 1 tablespoon butter and the mushrooms and cook for another 2 minutes. Add the soy sauce and bread crumbs; season with salt and pepper. Let cool.

4. Make half the recipe for pierogi dough. Follow only step 1, and then divide the dough into two equal pieces. Working with one piece at a time on a lightly floured surface, use a rolling pin to roll out the dough to a thickness of just less than ⅛ inch (3 mm), lifting up the dough to dust the work surface with flour and prevent sticking if needed. Using a small pastry cutter or inverted glass tumbler, cut out 2-inch (5 cm) circles of dough. By hand, roll out every circle even thinner, around 2½ inches (6 cm) thick. Repeat with the other piece of dough and the combined scraps.

5. Put ½ teaspoon filling in the center of each round. Grasp the dough from opposite ends to pull up and over the filling, then press the edges to seal and create a semicircle. Pinch to seal completely (if the edges don't adhere, lightly brush with water, then seal). Bring the opposite ends of the dumpling toward each other and press together (it will resemble a ring); do not leave any gaps, or the pierogi may open while cooking. Continue until all the dough is used.

6. Boil a large pot of water with salt and the oil. Working in batches, use a slotted spoon to gently lower 10 to 15 *uszka* at a time into the pot. Cook for 2 minutes, or until they float to the surface, then remove from the water immediately with a slotted spoon. Serve with *Barszcz czysty czerwony*.

Notes: *For the filling, you can instead use the mushrooms left over from* Barszcz czysty czerwony *(Clear Fermented Beet Soup, page 78).*

Liquid left over after cooking mushrooms is such an umami shot. You can use this mushroom bouillon to cook a soup, for example.

KOPYTKA
with Mushroom-Mustard Sauce
Kopytka w sosie grzybowym z musztardą

Kopytka literally means "little hooves," because, apparently, they look like them. I think these simple potato dumplings actually look more like diamonds. *Kopytka* are Polish gnocchi, and they're a little more rustic than the Italian version. The secret to good *kopytka* is to boil potatoes in their skins, so they won't absorb too much water and you can add less flour for softer, lighter dumplings. Feel free to add more or less flour to get the dough to feel soft and not too sticky. You can serve them just with butter and herbs, or with an earthy mushroom sauce spiked with vodka and mustard. It's the best comfort food ever.

MAKES	PREP TIME	COOK TIME
4 servings	10 minutes	1 hour

FOR THE DUMPLINGS

1 pound (450 g) small Yukon Gold potatoes

1 large egg

1 cup (130 g) all-purpose flour, plus more for dusting

Salt

FOR THE SAUCE

3 tablespoons (45 g) unsalted butter

10½ ounces (300 g) fresh mushrooms, preferably porcini or cremini, sliced into quarters

¼ cup (60 ml) bison grass vodka or herbal vodka

1 cup (220 ml) heavy cream

2 tablespoons whole grain mustard

1 teaspoon honey

Freshly ground black pepper

Chopped fresh parsley

1. **To make the dumplings,** cook the potatoes in their skins in a large pot of boiling water over medium-high heat until fork-tender, 30 to 40 minutes. Drain the potatoes and let cool. As soon as the potatoes are cool enough to handle, peel and mash them with a potato masher. Let cool.

2. Put the cold mashed potatoes in a large bowl. Add the egg and stir to combine. Add the flour and 1 teaspoon salt and stir to combine. Turn out the dough onto a floured surface and gently knead, dusting with more flour as needed, until the dough is smooth but not elastic, about 2 minutes. Be careful not to overwork it, to avoid a tough dough.

3. Divide the dough into four equal pieces. Roll each piece into a 20-inch-long (50 cm) rope about ½ inch (1.25 cm) thick. Working with one rope at a time, cut the dough at an angle into ½-inch (1.25 cm) pieces; dust with more flour if needed.

4. Bring a large pot of salted water to a boil. Working in batches, drop the dumplings into the boiling water and cook until they float to the surface, about 2 minutes. Using a slotted spoon, transfer the cooked dumplings to a colander to drain. Repeat until all the dumplings have been cooked. Reserve about 1 cup of the dumpling cooking water.

5. **To make the sauce,** heat the butter in a large skillet over medium-high heat. Add the mushrooms and sauté until tender and golden, about 7 minutes. Add the vodka and stir until it has evaporated, about 30 seconds. Add the cream, mustard, and honey, and stir to combine. Cook, uncovered, until the sauce is thickens slightly, about 2 minutes.

6. Add the cooked dumplings and ½ cup of the reserved dumpling water to the skillet with the mushroom sauce. Toss over medium heat until heated through, coating the *kopytka* with the sauce. Season with salt and pepper, top with parsley, and serve.

Note: You can also serve kopytka *without sauce, as a side dish. They taste even more comforting fried in a bit of butter the next day.*

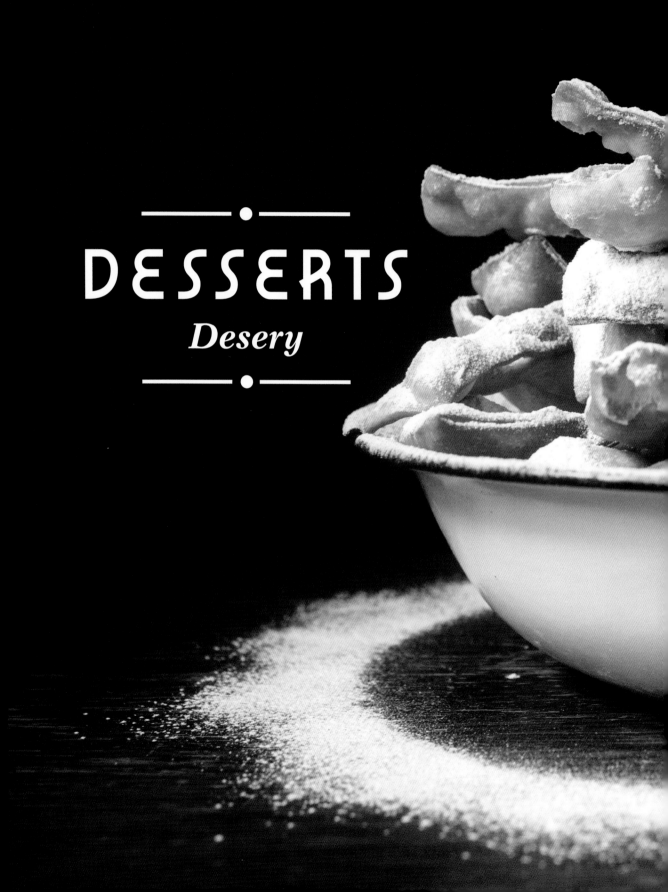

DESSERTS

Desery

I can't lie—this is my favorite chapter. I have the biggest sweet tooth and a second stomach for dessert, and Polish desserts are truly magnificent. We start with *Sernik* (Traditional Polish Cheesecake, page 180), since there's no place in the world where cheesecakes taste as good as along the Wisła river. And this chapter includes *Pączki z konfiturą różaną i cytrynowym lukrem* (*Pączki* with Rose Petal Preserves and Lemon Glaze, page 190), yeasted donuts topped with candied orange zest. There are so many amazing desserts—I can never decide what I want to bake. And I can bake without ever taking a break.

I turned my love of sweets into a job. As a teenager, I got a job as a confectioner at a local pastry shop in my hometown. I remember how excited I was the day before my interview, when, unable to fall asleep, I couldn't stop thinking about what they would ask me to bake. Would it be simple cookies, or maybe more advanced multilayered cakes? In the morning, I showed up at the door of a small, cozy bakery in the suburbs of my hometown of Rzeszów. My hair was ruffled, shoelaces loose, and I was still breathing heavily after my long bike trip. Three older ladies with round, sympathetic faces gave me piercing looks full of doubt. One of them asked politely if I was Michał and if I would be working with them. "Yes, it's me," I quickly answered. Another one, sighing, added, "You are small, one-third the size of me," and then asked me to make a cheesecake. This huge cheesecake was made with 11 pounds of *twaróg*, 40 eggs, and a ton of raisins soaked in lots of rum. I separated the whites from the yolks, with the fear that I would accidentally include a whole egg with the whites, so it wouldn't be possible to beat them into a stiff foam. Lucky for me, it didn't happen. Actually, the cheesecake turned out perfect. My new colleagues praised its fluffiness and lightness—and they hired me on the spot.

TRADITIONAL POLISH CHEESECAKE

Sernik

There's no dessert more Polish than *sernik,* which is served at every family gathering and on Christmas. But as a child, I hated it. Traditionally, *sernik* contains raisins, which, in my opinion, are the worst food ever. When I finally tried a version without them, I fell in love. There's a huge difference between a cream cheese–based New York–style cheesecake and a *twaróg*-based *sernik.* The first is rich and smooth, and has a creamy consistency, but the second is lighter in texture and delightfully fluffy with a play of sour and sweet. Now you can try them for yourself and choose which is best.

MAKES	PREP TIME	COOK TIME
12 servings	20 minutes	2 hours

FOR THE CRUST

1¼ cups (160 g) all-purpose flour

⅓ cup (75 g) sugar

¼ teaspoon kosher salt

½ cup (1 stick/115 g) unsalted butter, cut into pieces

FOR THE FILLING

¾ cup (1½ sticks/170 g) unsalted butter

1¼ cups (150 g) powdered sugar, plus more for serving

2 vanilla beans, split lengthwise, or 1 tablespoon pure vanilla extract

5 large eggs, yolks and whites separated

1 pound 11 ounces (760 g) full-fat farmer cheese, *Twaróg* (page 44), or dry-curd cottage cheese, passed through a sieve or blended until smooth

⅔ cup (160 ml) heavy cream

3 tablespoons cornstarch

1. **To make the crust,** whisk together the all-purpose flour, sugar, and salt. Add the butter, then use your fingers to rub it into the flour mixture to make a light bread-crumb texture. Chill in the fridge for at least 30 minutes, or until the dough is firm.

2. Meanwhile, preheat the oven to 350°F (180°C).

3. Transfer the crust to a 9-inch (23 cm) springform pan. Using the bottom of a measuring cup, press the crumbs firmly into the pan. Bake until the crust is fragrant and the edges just start to brown, 15 to 20 minutes. Transfer the pan to a wire rack and let cool. Leave the oven on.

4. **To make the filling,** in the bowl of a stand mixer fitted with a paddle attachment, beat the butter on medium speed until smooth, about 40 seconds. Add the sugar, increase the speed to medium-high, and beat until very light and fluffy, about 5 minutes. Scrape in the vanilla bean seeds or vanilla extract (save the pods for another use). Reduce the speed to medium and add the egg yolks one at a time, beating as you add each yolk. Add the cheese, cream, and cornstarch; continue to mix until smooth.

5. In a separate clean bowl, beat the egg whites to stiff peaks. Fold them into the filling.

6. Scrape the filling into the cooled crust. Put it in the oven and immediately reduce the heat to 325°F (160°C). Bake until the edges are set but the center is still quite wobbly and the top of the cheesecake is slightly golden, about 1 hour. Turn off the heat and let the cake cool in the oven with the door propped open for 30 minutes. Transfer the pan to a wire rack and let cool completely before serving. Dust with powdered sugar and serve at room temperature.

Note: If your sernik cracks a bit, don't be scared. It happens. You always can top it with a lot of fresh berries, and the taste will be even more delightful.

YEAST *ROGALIKI*
with Rose Petal Preserves
Drożdżowe rogaliki z konfiturą różaną

I have a sweet tooth, and my brother is my total opposite. He hates cakes, cookies, and all baked goods with one exception: soft, yeasted *rogaliki* filled with rose petal preserves. If I need his help with anything, I just promise him a batch and he's there. *Rogaliki* is an adaptation of Jewish rugelach, which are more common in the United States. Those have a cream cheese dough, which lends them their intense flakiness; in Polish bakeries, you'll find yeast-leavened ones like these, which are soft and light.

MAKES	PREP TIME	RISING TIME	BAKE TIME
16 *rogaliki*	30 minutes	1 hour	15 minutes

1¾ cups (220 g) all-purpose flour

One ¼-ounce (7 g) packet instant yeast

3 tablespoons sugar

1 teaspoon grated lemon zest

¼ teaspoon salt

¼ cup (60 ml) warm milk

¼ cup (½ stick/60 g) unsalted butter, melted

2 tablespoons sour cream

1 large egg, lightly beaten

½ cup (150 g) rose petal preserves

1 egg yolk

1 tablespoon milk

Powdered sugar

1. **To make the dough,** combine the flour, yeast, sugar, lemon zest, and salt in the bowl of a stand mixer fitted with a dough hook. Add the warm milk, butter, sour cream, and egg. Mix on medium speed for 1 minute, or until just combined. Knead on medium-high speed until the dough is soft and silky, about 6 minutes. Cover with plastic wrap and let the dough sit in a warm place until it has tripled in volume, 40 to 60 minutes.

2. Line a baking sheet with parchment paper. Lightly flour a work surface and turn the dough out onto it. Sprinkle the dough with a little more flour and fold it over onto itself twice. Divide the dough into two parts. Working with one part at a time, roll it out into a 10-inch (25 cm) circle. Cut the circle into 8 wedges. Place 1 teaspoon of the jam along the outer, rounded rim of each wedge. Then, holding the tip of the opposite corner down, roll the outer edge over the filling toward the tip until it forms a tight roll. Place on the baking sheet; repeat with remaining wedges and preserves.

recipe continues . . .

3. Beat the egg yolk and milk together in a small bowl. Gently brush the egg wash on the *rogaliki;* refrigerate any remaining egg wash. Let the rogaliki sit until puffed, 20 to 30 minutes.

4. Meanwhile, preheat the oven to 350°F (180°C).

5. Brush the *rogaliki* with more egg wash. Bake until golden brown, 15 to 20 minutes. Dust with the powdered sugar. Let cool before serving. Store at room temperature, wrapped in plastic.

   Note: *Rose petal preserves are a typical Polish filling for the* rogaliki, *but you can use your favorite fruit jam or sweet spread.*

CRANBERRY–COTTAGE CHEESE CHEESECAKE

Żurawionowy sernik na serkach wiejskich

While I was working on this cookbook, I struggled with how to present the *twaróg*-based recipes, to keep them fully authentic yet accessible for people who don't have access to Polish delis. I tried many, many kinds of white cheese! Eventually I landed on a decent substitute for *twaróg*: small-curd cottage cheese. *Sernik* (Traditional Polish Cheesecake, page 180) is truly one of a kind, but this cheesecake is also delicious. The flavor is milkier and delicate but still has a bit of sourness as true farmer cheese should.

MAKES	PREP TIME	BAKE TIME	CHILLING TIME
12 servings	30 minutes	45 minutes	2 hours

FOR THE CRUST

1¼ cups (160 g) all-purpose flour

⅓ cup (75 g) sugar

¼ teaspoon kosher salt

½ cup (1 stick/115 g) unsalted butter, cut into pieces

FOR THE FILLING

2¾ cups (620 g) small-curd cottage cheese

¼ cup (60 ml) heavy cream

½ cup (1 stick/115 g) unsalted butter, room temperature

½ cup (120 g) powdered sugar

5 large eggs, yolks and whites separated

2 tablespoons finely grated orange zest

1 tablespoon cornstarch

FOR THE TOPPING

12 ounces (3½ cups/360 g) fresh or thawed frozen cranberries

¾ cup (150 g) sugar

Juice of 1 orange

1. **To make the crust,** whisk together the all-purpose flour, sugar, and salt. Add the butter, then use your fingers to rub it into the flour to make a light bread-crumb texture. Chill in the fridge for at least 30 minutes, or until the dough is firm.

2. Meanwhile, preheat the oven to 350°F (180°C).

3. Transfer the crust crumbs to a 9-inch (23 cm) springform pan. Using the bottom of a measuring cup, press the crumbs firmly into the pan. Bake until the crust is fragrant and the edges just start to brown, about 20 minutes. Transfer the pan to a wire rack and let cool. Leave the oven on.

4. **To make the filling,** use an immersion blender to blend the cottage cheese with the heavy cream into a smooth purée. In the bowl of a stand mixer fitted with a paddle attachment, beat the butter on medium speed until smooth, about 40 seconds. Add the powdered sugar, increase the speed to medium-high, and beat until very light and fluffy, about 5 minutes. Reduce the speed to medium and add the egg yolks one at a time, beating as you add each yolk. Add the cottage cheese purée, orange zest, and cornstarch; mix until smooth.

5. Meanwhile, in a separate clean bowl, beat the egg whites to stiff peaks. Fold them into the filling very gently.

6. Scrape the filling into the cooled crust. Put in the oven and immediately reduce the heat to 325°F (160°C). Bake until the edges are set but the center is still quite wobbly, and the top of the cheesecake is slightly golden, about 45 minutes. Turn off the heat and let the cake cool in the oven with the door propped open for 30 minutes. Transfer the pan to a wire rack and let cool completely.

7. Meanwhile, make the topping. Bring the cranberries, sugar, and orange juice to a boil in a medium saucepan over medium-high heat. Reduce the heat and simmer until the cranberries mostly burst, 6 to 8 minutes. Let cool. Top the cooled cheesecake with the cranberry sauce. Chill until firm, at least 2 hours.

Note: To avoid gummy and messy slices of cake, dip your knife in hot water and wipe it clean before every single cut.

YEAST-BUTTERMILK CAKE
with Berries and Streusel
Ciasto drożdżowe na maślance z owocami i kruszonką

There is nothing quite like the glorious smell of yeast cake baking in the oven. My mom always says that the smell turns the house into a paradise. She really loves yeasty, sweet treats, so good son that I am, I often bake this cake for her. My version combines a rich buttermilk dough with the refreshing flavors of berries and the crunch of buttery streusel topping. Drizzle this heavenly, fluffy cake with honey or powdered sugar and watch how quickly it disappears.

MAKES	PREP TIME	RISING TIME	COOK TIME
16 servings	20 minutes	1½ hours	35 minutes

FOR THE DOUGH

4 cups (520 g) all-purpose flour

Two ¼-ounce (14 g total) packets instant yeast

½ cup (100 g) sugar

½ teaspoon kosher salt

2 large eggs, lightly beaten

1 cup plus 1 tablespoon (250 ml) full-fat buttermilk

¾ cup (1½ sticks/175 g) unsalted butter, melted, plus more for the pan

Sunflower oil

1 pound (450 g) berries or sliced pitted stone fruits (I like a mix of peaches, nectarines, and plums)

FOR THE STREUSEL TOPPING

1¼ cups (160 g) all-purpose flour

⅓ cup (75 g) sugar

¼ cup plus 1 tablespoon (75 g) unsalted butter, chilled and cut into pieces

1. **To make the dough,** combine the flour, sugar, yeast, and salt in the bowl of a stand mixer fitted with a dough hook. Add the eggs, buttermilk, and melted butter. Mix on medium speed for 1 minute, or until combined. Knead on medium-high speed until the dough is soft and silky, 10 to 15 minutes. When you push down on it, the dough should feel firm and elastic.

2. Transfer the dough to a large oiled bowl. Cover with plastic wrap and let it sit in a warm place until the dough has tripled in volume, about 1½ hours. To test if the dough has fully risen, make an indentation with your finger in the center of the dough. If the indentation remains, move on to the next step. If not, continue to let it rise.

3. Meanwhile, make the streusel topping. Whisk together the all-purpose flour and sugar. Add the butter, then use your fingers to rub it into the flour to make a light bread-crumb texture. Chill in the fridge for at least 30 minutes, or until firm.

4. Lightly butter a 9 x 13-inch (23 x 33 cm) pan and line it with parchment paper. Scrape the dough into the pan and smooth the top with your hands. Scatter the berries over the dough. Cover the pan with plastic wrap and let sit at room temperature until it doubles in volume, about 25 minutes.

5. Meanwhile, preheat the oven to 350°F (180°C).

6. Sprinkle the streusel topping over the cake. Bake for about 35 minutes, until a toothpick inserted into the center comes out clean and the top is golden. Let cool before serving. Store at room temperature, wrapped in plastic.

PĄCZKI
with Rose Petal Preserves and Lemon Glaze
Pączki z konfiturą różaną i cytrynowym lukrem

There is a vibrant tradition of eating *pączki* (donuts) in Poland. We've eaten *pączki* since the Middle Ages, and they even have their own feast—Fat Thursday—when everybody eats as many as they can. A perfect donut should be still warm and very fluffy, well-fried but not burnt, and with a bright stripe around the center. The glaze should glitter and stick to your fingers. When it comes to the filling, I am not a purist. I find it easier to stuff a *pączek* after frying, filling it with a lavish amount of rose petal preserves.

MAKES	PREP TIME	RISING TIME	COOK TIME
14 donuts	40 minutes	1½ to 2 hours	15 minutes

FOR THE DOUGH

3½ cups (450 g) all-purpose flour, plus more for shaping

Two ¼-ounce (14 g total) packets instant yeast

⅓ cup (70 g) sugar

½ teaspoon salt

¾ cup (180 ml) lukewarm milk

¼ cup (½ stick/60 g) unsalted butter, melted

2 large eggs

1 egg yolk

3 tablespoons dark rum

Vegetable oil

FOR FILLING AND ASSEMBLY

1 pound (1½ cups/450 g) rose petal preserves

¼ cup (60 ml) fresh lemon juice (about 2 lemons)

2 cups (260 g) powdered sugar

3 tablespoons dried rose petals

1. Combine the flour, yeast, sugar, and salt in the bowl of a stand mixer fitted with a dough hook. Add the milk, butter, eggs, egg yolk, and rum. Mix on medium speed for 1 minute, or until combined. Knead on medium-high speed until the dough is soft and silky, about 6 minutes. Cover with plastic wrap and let sit at room temperature until the dough has doubled in volume, 1 to 1½ hours.

2. Turn the dough out onto a floured surface. Divide into 14 pieces (about 2½ ounces/70 g each), then shape into balls. Put the *pączki* on two floured baking sheets so that there is plenty of room between them. Cover with a kitchen towel and let rise at room temperature until they are slightly puffed up and delicate, about 30 minutes.

3. About 15 minutes before the doughnuts are done rising, put the oil in a heavy-bottomed pot or Dutch oven over medium heat to a depth of 4 inches (10 cm) and heat to 350°F (175°C). Line a plate with paper towels.

4. Working in batches, fry the *pączki* until golden, 1 to 2 minutes per side. Transfer to the plate and let cool slightly before filling.

5. Scrape the preserves into a piping bag fitted with a ¼- to ½-inch (6 to 12 mm) tip. You can fill the *pączki* from the top or side. Press the tip of the bag halfway into the *pączek* and gently squeeze in jam until it just pokes out of the hole. Repeat with remaining *pączki*.

6. **To make the glaze,** heat the lemon juice in a small saucepan over low heat. Remove from the heat, then stir in the powdered sugar until well combined. Drizzle the glaze over the *pączki;* top with rose petals. Serve immediately.

Note: The most traditional filling for pączki *is rose petal preserves, but try a version with your favorite fruit jam, chocolate spread, or vanilla custard.*

HEAVEN CAKE

Niebo w gębie

At my grandma Zosia's house, no matter how many modern, surprising, or delicious cakes appear on the table, this old-fashioned cake always has the most admirers. It's like a family secret: My grandma can't even tell me the recipe, because she doesn't know it—she makes everything by instinct. For this cake, you have to spend some time in the kitchen, because the cake has five layers (chocolate glaze also counts!). But good things come to those who wait: Tart apples are stiffened with agar and placed between two layers of shortcrust pastry, followed by buttery walnut cream, which melts in the mouth. Bittersweet chocolate ganache is spread over the entire thing. I can never eat just one slice.

MAKES	PREP TIME	CHILLING TIME	BAKE TIME	COOK TIME
18 servings	40 minutes	4½ to 5½ hours	30 minutes	1½ hours

FOR THE CRUST

3 cups (390 g) all-purpose flour

⅔ cup (100 g) powdered sugar

¼ teaspoon salt

1¼ cup (2½ sticks/280 g) unsalted butter, chilled and cubed

3 egg yolks

FOR THE APPLE FILLING

3 pounds (1350 g) Granny Smith apples, peeled, cored, and cut into ¼- to ½-inch (8 mm) cubes

3 tablespoons fresh lemon juice

⅓ cup (75 g) agar

1 tablespoon finely grated lemon zest

FOR THE BUTTER-WALNUT CREAM

1 cup (240 ml) milk

2½ cups (250 g) finely ground walnuts

1 cup (120 g) powdered sugar

¼ teaspoon salt

1 cup (2 sticks/230 g) unsalted butter, at room temperature

3 tablespoons dark rum

FOR THE GANACHE

½ cup (120 ml) heavy cream

3½ ounces (100 g) dark chocolate, chopped

1. **To make the crust,** whisk together the all-purpose flour, sugar, and salt. Add the butter, then use your fingers to rub it into the flour to make a light bread-crumb texture. Add the egg yolks and toss with a fork until moist clumps form. Gather the dough into two equal balls, then flatten each into a disk. Wrap in plastic, then chill in the fridge for at least 30 minutes, until the dough is firm.

2. Roll out one piece of the dough on lightly floured parchment paper to a 9 x 13-inch (23 x 33 cm) rectangle. Transfer it, still on the parchment paper, to a 9 x 13-inch (23 x 33 cm) baking pan. Chill until firm, about 30 minutes.

3. Meanwhile, preheat the oven to 375°F (190°C).

recipe continues . . .

4. Bake until golden brown, about 15 minutes. Transfer to a wire rack, on the parchment paper, and let cool. Repeat rolling, chilling, and baking the second piece of dough.

5. While the crust layers are baking and cooling, make the apple filling. Combine the apples and lemon juice in a large saucepan; cook until the apples are soft and starting to break apart into applesauce. Remove from the heat. Stir in the agar and lemon zest. Let cool completely.

6. **To make the butter-walnut cream,** bring the milk to a boil in a medium saucepan. Stir in the ground walnuts and salt and cook until thick, 3 to 4 minutes. Let cool completely.

7. Beat the butter with sugar for 2 to 3 minutes, until pale and fluffy. Stirring constantly, add 1 tablespoon of the walnut cream at a time, until the mixtures are combined.

8. Return a layer of crust to the baking pan. Spread on the apple filling, then top with the second layer of crust. Spread the butter-walnut cream on top. Chill in the fridge for at least 2 to 3 hours.

9. **To make the ganache,** bring the cream to a boil in a medium saucepan. Remove from the heat; cool slightly. Add the chocolate; stir constantly until smooth. Spread over the cake. Chill in the fridge until set, about 1 hour.

10. About 30 minutes before serving, remove the cake from the fridge to soften it a bit. Store in the fridge, wrapped in plastic, for up to 3 days.

ROSE *MAZUREK*
with Almonds
Różany mazurek z migdałami

Mazurek is a folk dance (known in English as the mazurka), a beautiful lake region, and a flat shortcrust pastry topped with chocolate or the caramel cream *kajmak* (dulce de leche) that's frequently baked for Easter. In this recipe, you'll beat the cream with rose petal preserves and sweeten the crust with almonds, giving a delightful twist to an old tradition. Every bite is heavenly and full of floral notes that will take your breath away.

MAKES	PREP TIME	CHILLING TIME	BAKE TIME
15 servings	20 minutes	1½ hours	25 minutes

FOR THE CRUST

1½ cups (200 g) all-purpose flour

⅓ cup (40 g) ground almonds

2 tablespoons cornstarch

3 tablespoons powdered sugar

¼ teaspoon salt

½ cup plus 2 tablespoons (1¼ sticks/150 g) chilled unsalted butter, cut into pieces

2 egg yolks

FOR FILLING AND ASSEMBLY

½ cup (150 g) rose petal preserves

1 cup (230 g) mascarpone cheese

½ cup raspberry jam

1 cup (70 g) slivered almonds

3 tablespoons dried rose petals and a few unsprayed rose petals, for serving (optional)

1. **To make the crust,** whisk the flour, ground almonds, cornstarch, powdered sugar, and salt in a medium bowl. Add the butter and toss to coat. Using your fingers, smash the butter into dry ingredients until it nearly disappears. Add the egg yolks; toss with a fork until moist clumps form. Gather the dough into a ball, then flatten into a disk. Wrap in plastic and chill for 1 hour in the fridge until firm.

2. Roll out the dough on lightly floured parchment paper to a 9 x 13-inch (23 x 33 cm) rectangle. Transfer, still on the parchment paper, to a rimmed baking sheet. Using a sharp knife, lightly score about a ½-inch (1.25 cm) border around the edge of the dough. Chill in the fridge until firm, about 30 minutes.

3. While the dough is chilling, preheat the oven to 375°F (190°C). Bake until golden brown, 20 to 25 minutes. Transfer to a wire rack and let cool.

4. **To make the filling,** place the rose petal preserves and mascarpone in the bowl of a stand mixer fitted with a paddle attachment and beat until fluffy and combined, 1 to 2 minutes.

5. Spread the raspberry jam over the baked crust. Top it with the rose-mascarpone filling, and then the slivered almonds. You can decorate this *mazurek* with rose petals, if desired, for a charming effect. Store in the fridge, wrapped in plastic, for up to 2 days.

   Note: Using rose petal preserves is essential. You can get it in well-stocked delis or online.

LEMON-VANILLA *KARPATKA*
with Crunchy Topping

Karpatka z cytrynowo-waniliowym kremem i chrupiącą skorupką

Everybody loves this old-fashioned cake. It starts with two simple choux pastry layers, which puff dramatically, resembling the Polish Karpaty mountains. These are filled with butter pastry cream, which I like to improve with tangy lemon zest and vanilla. But choux pastry gets soggy in time. To keep it crunchy for longer, I cover the cake with a sugar-butter-flour topping; this also makes it look like a bird's-eye view of the mountain forest. I fell in love with *karpatka* in childhood so much that I would ask my mom if she would make it for my birthday instead of a cake. I was delighted with a tower of *karpatka* pieces filled lavishly with butter pastry cream, which was my weakness. And probably still is.

MAKES	PREP TIME	CHILLING TIME	BAKE TIME
15 pastries	2½ hours	1½ hours	30 minutes

FOR THE CRUNCHY TOPPING

½ cup (1 stick/115 g) unsalted butter

½ cup (100 g) sugar

1 cup (130 g) all-purpose flour

½ teaspoon grated lemon zest

¼ teaspoon salt

FOR THE CHOUX PASTRY

1 cup (130 g) all-purpose flour

1 teaspoon baking powder

1 teaspoon sugar

¼ teaspoon salt

½ cup (1 stick/115 g) unsalted butter, plus more for the pans

5 large eggs

FOR THE BUTTER PASTRY CREAM

2½ cups (600 ml) milk

2 tablespoons grated lemon zest

1 vanilla bean, split lengthwise

3 egg yolks

½ cup (100 g) sugar

3 tablespoons cornstarch

1 tablespoon fresh lemon juice

½ pound (2 sticks/230 g) unsalted butter

1. **To make the topping,** beat the butter with the sugar in a medium bowl. Add the flour, lemon zest, and salt. Put the dough between two sheets of parchment paper and roll it until it is very thin, about ⅒ inch (2.5 mm) thick. Place it, still between the sheets of parchment paper, on a baking sheet and freeze for 30 minutes, or until set.

2. While the topping is chilling, preheat the oven to 400°F (200°C). Butter two 9 x 13-inch (23 x 33 cm) baking pans, then line them with parchment paper.

3. **To make the choux pastry,** combine the flour, baking powder, sugar, and salt in a small bowl. Bring 1 cup water to a boil with the butter in a medium saucepan, stirring occasionally. Add the flour mixture all at once and stir with a wooden spoon, carefully at first, to incorporate, then vigorously, until the dough forms a single mass. Continue until a film forms on the bottom of the saucepan, 1 to 2 minutes. (It's important to cook the flour and dry out the dough.) Remove from the heat.

4. Transfer the dough to the bowl of a stand mixer fitted with the paddle attachment and beat for 1 to 2 minutes, until the dough cools a bit. Mix the eggs into the dough one at a time, making sure to completely incorporate each egg before adding the next. The dough should be smooth and shiny.

5. Divide the dough between the prepared pans in even layers with a rubber spatula. Carefully place the frozen topping on one of them. (You can break it into pieces if necessary to cover the entire surface.) Transfer the pans to the oven and bake for 25 to 30 minutes, until unevenly puffed and deep golden brown. They should look like mountains. Remove from the oven and let cool.

6. **To make the pastry cream,** place the milk and the lemon zest in a medium saucepan, then scrape in the vanilla seeds and add the pods. Bring to a simmer over medium heat, then remove the vanilla pods. Meanwhile, whisk the egg yolks with the sugar in a medium bowl until very pale and fluffy, about 2 minutes. Add the cornstarch, whisking until no powdery dry spots remain. Whisking constantly, add 1 cup of the hot milk to the egg mixture, then pour everything back into the saucepan. Cook over medium heat, whisking constantly, until the mixture is thick and holds whisk marks, 2 to 3 minutes. Remove from the heat and stir in the lemon juice. Cover with plastic wrap, pressing it directly onto the surface. Let cool completely.

7. Beat the butter in a stand mixer until pale. Beat the pastry cream for 30 seconds, just to make it fluffier, then mix it into the butter, adding 1 tablespoon at a time and making sure to completely incorporate each portion before adding the next.

8. Spread the pastry cream on the pastry layer without the topping. Place the layer with the topping on top. Chill for 1 hour, until the cream sets. Dust with the powdered sugar. Serve immediately.

   Note: Karpatka tastes the best the day you make it, but you can store it for up to 2 days, covered and refrigerated.

HONEY CAKE
with Prunes and Sour Cream
Miodownik z kremem z kwaśnej śmietany i suszonymi śliwkami

One day, my friend Zosia and I were sauntering around the city of Lviv when it started raining. We found shelter in a buzzy cafe and ordered two coffees and one honey cake to share. I plunged the fork into all seven layers, slathered with glossy sour cream frosting and dried plums, and after the first bite, I asked the waitress for another piece. The cake seemed simple, but those few components merged to release a wave of sour, honey, bittersweet, and delightfully tangy notes with each bite. I knew that I had to figure out this recipe. So I spent hours in my kitchen, each failure bringing me closer to the perfection I remembered. And here we are.

MAKES	PREP TIME	CHILLING TIME	BAKE TIME
16 servings	40 minutes	12 hours	10 minutes

FOR THE HONEY CAKE

¾ cup (270 ml) honey

1¼ cup (2½ sticks/280 g) unsalted butter

¾ cup (140 g) Demerara or brown sugar

3 cups (390 g) all-purpose flour

1 teaspoon ground cinnamon

2½ teaspoons baking powder

¾ teaspoon salt

4 large eggs, lightly beaten

FOR THE FROSTING

1½ tablespoons agar

4 cups (900 g) sour cream

1 cup (220 g) heavy cream

½ cup (60 g) powdered sugar

2 cups (300 g) prunes, pitted and chopped

FOR THE SOAK

¼ cup (85 g) honey

¼ cup (60 ml) dark rum

Powdered sugar

1. Preheat the oven to 350°F (180°C). Line two 9-inch (23 cm) round cake pans with parchment paper.

2. **To make the honey cake,** melt the honey, butter, and sugar in a medium saucepan. Remove from the heat and set aside for 15 minutes, until cool.

3. Place the flour, cinnamon, baking powder, and salt into a large bowl. Stir the eggs into the honey mixture, then pour into the flour mixture and beat until smooth.

4. Divide the batter between the prepared pans. Bake for 30 to 40 minutes, until the cakes turn a deep caramel color and spring back at the touch. A skewer pushed into the center of a cake should come out clean. Let cool in the pans briefly, then turn out onto a wire rack to cool completely.

5. Use a serrated knife to halve the cakes horizontally, moving it back and forth in long, even strokes. If needed, trim the dome from the top of each cake to create a flat surface. You can save the crumbs for decoration.

6. **To make the frosting,** place 3 tablespoons cold water in a small saucepan and sprinkle the agar evenly over the top. Chill for about 10 minutes, until the agar has softened. Heat over medium-low heat, swirling the pan often, until the agar dissolves, about 1 minute. Stir in 2 tablespoons of the sour cream.

7. Beat the heavy cream in the bowl of a stand mixer fitted with a whisk attachment on medium-high speed until medium peaks form. Add the powdered sugar and the rest of the sour cream. Beat for 3 minutes, until well combined.

8. Stream the agar mixture into the whipped cream, still beating. Add the prunes; stir to combine. Chill for 30 minutes, until the frosting sets.

9. To make the soak, heat the honey and rum in a saucepan over medium heat. Let cool.

10. Assemble the cake on a 10-inch (25 cm) cardboard circle or flat serving plate. Place a cake layer in the center of the cardboard, then, using a spoon, spread one quarter of the soak over the cake layer. Spoon one quarter of the frosting onto the center. Use an offset spatula to spread the frosting evenly, leaving a ¼-inch (6 mm) border around the edge. Place the next cake layer atop the frosting, center it, soak, and frost. Continue as above with the remaining cake layers, soak, and frosting. Cover with plastic and chill for at least 12 hours. Dust with the powdered sugar.

Note: Store this in the fridge for up to 5 days. With each day the cake tastes better.

COCOA-CHILE CAKE
with Chocolate Frosting
Ciasto czekoladowe z chili

This cocoa cake, without a gram of chocolate, is a relic of past times when a chocolate bar was too luxurious to afford. It isn't a fudgy, dense brownie, but a moist pound cake, perfect for evening tea or even a sweet supper. My mom used to make it for me after a long day of school. She dusted warm cocoa slices with powdered sugar, and I ate a lot of them. Nowadays, I like to stir a few chile flakes into the batter for a little punch. What's more, the cake is served with a chocolate frosting made with sweetened condensed milk.

MAKES	PREP TIME	BAKE TIME
8 servings	15 minutes	40 minutes

FOR THE CAKE
Unsalted butter

1¾ cups (230 g) all-purpose flour, plus more for the pan

½ cup (60 g) unsweetened cocoa powder

1⅓ cups (270 g) sugar

1¼ teaspoons baking powder

1 teaspoon salt

½ teaspoon chile flakes (optional)

½ cup (120 ml) extra virgin olive oil

1 teaspoon pure vanilla extract

2 large eggs, at room temperature

FOR THE FROSTING
¾ cup (180 ml) heavy cream

½ cup (150 g) sweetened condensed milk

7 ounces (170 g) dark chocolate, chopped

¼ teaspoon salt

¼ cup (½ stick/60 g) unsalted butter, chilled and cubed

1. Preheat the oven to 350°F (180°C). Lightly butter and flour a 10 x 5-inch (26 x 12 cm) loaf pan.

2. **To make the cake,** whisk together the cocoa powder, flour, sugar, baking powder, salt, and chile flakes, if using, in a medium bowl.

3. Bring 1½ cups (360 ml) water to a boil in a small saucepan, then add the olive oil and vanilla. Gradually stir this into the cocoa mixture until incorporated. Whisk in the eggs. Stir until batter is smooth and thin.

4. Pour the batter into the prepared pan. Bake until a toothpick inserted into the center comes out clean, about 50 minutes. Transfer the pan to a wire rack; let cool in the pan for 15 minutes and then turn out onto the wire rack to cool completely. (It should not be warm to the touch, or else the icing will melt when you spread it on.)

5. While the cake is baking, make the chocolate frosting. Combine the cream, condensed milk, chocolate, and salt in a medium saucepan. Cook over low heat, stirring occasionally, until the mixture begins to boil. Remove from the heat. Add the chilled butter and blend with an immersion blender until smooth. Transfer to jars or a bowl and chill in the fridge until set.

6. Smooth the frosting over top of the cake. Serve with more frosting on the side, spreading it lavishly on every bite. Store in the fridge, wrapped in plastic, for up to 3 days (bring cake to room temperature before serving). The frosting, covered, will keep in the fridge up to 1 week.

ANGEL WINGS
with Cardamom Sugar
Faworki z kardamonowym cukrem

Faworki are like crispy puffs of air dusted with powdered sugar. They are one of my favorite treats that appear in shop windows during Carnival. People in Poland are strict about eating these only during this special time, but I see no reason why you can't make a few *faworki* whenever you want. Serve them with cardamom sugar for an even more delightful experience.

MAKES	PREP TIME	COOK TIME
about 50 pieces	30 minutes	20 minutes

3 egg yolks

⅓ cup plus 1 tablespoon (50 g) powdered sugar

3 tablespoons sour cream

1 teaspoon vodka

1½ cups (200 g) all-purpose flour, plus more for rolling

½ teaspoon grated lemon zest

½ teaspoon baking powder

¼ teaspoon salt

One 48-ounce (1.4 L) bottle vegetable oil, for frying

2 teaspoons ground cardamom

1. In a medium bowl, beat the egg yolks with 1 tablespoon of the powdered sugar until pale, about 4 minutes. Stir in the sour cream and vodka. Combine the flour, lemon zest, baking powder, and salt in another medium bowl; stir into the egg mixture. Mix until combined and soft, about 2 minutes.

2. Flour a work surface. Roll out the dough, fold it in half and roll out again. Repeat three more times. Divide the dough into two pieces and cover one with plastic wrap. Roll out the uncovered piece until it is very thin, about ½2 inch (2 mm) thick. Cut into 2-inch-wide (5 cm) strips. Cut these strips on the diagonal at 5-inch (12 cm) intervals. Make a slit lengthwise down the center of each strip of dough, then pull one end through the slit to form a bow. Repeat with the other piece of dough.

3. Heat the oil to 350°F (180°C) in a large skillet. Cover a big plate with several layers of paper towels. Fry a few dough pieces at a time, making sure not to crowd the pan, until golden, 1 to 2 minutes per side. Drain on the paper towels.

4. Combine the remaining ⅓ cup (40 g) powdered sugar with the cardamom. Dust the *faworki*. Serve immediately.

Note: Faworki are best served immediately after cooking but can be stored at room temperature for several days, gently covered with a kitchen towel or aluminum foil.

CHERRY LIQUEUR BABAS

Baby na wiśniówce

This beloved boozy treat—known as *baba au rhum* in France and *babà Napoletano al rum* in Italy—is made of small yeasted brioche-like cakes swimming in alcohol, and it's originally of Polish origin. It was introduced to France in the eighteenth century by Stanisław I, the exiled king of Poland. He had the idea to soak a dry yeast babka cake into some wine, just to have something to bite into while drinking. Soon after, it migrated all over the world. In Naples, they adapted it with limoncello, which gave me the idea to use my favorite Polish cherry liqueur, *wiśniówka*. This recipe has a delicate fruity flavor, with just a hint of alcohol and a buttery lightness.

MAKES	PREP TIME	RISING TIME	BAKE TIME	CHILLING TIME
8 babas	30 minutes	2 hours	30 to 40 minutes	1 to 2 hours

FOR THE BABAS

2½ cups (320 g) all-purpose flour, plus more for the cups

One ¼-ounce (7 g) packet instant yeast

¼ cup (50 g) sugar

¼ teaspoon salt

2 large eggs

⅓ cup plus 1 tablespoon (95 ml) milk

½ cup (1 stick/115 g) unsalted butter, melted

Vegetable oil or butter

1 egg yolk

FOR THE SYRUP

2 cups (480 ml) cherry liqueur, such as Soplica Wiśniowa

1 cup (200 g) sugar

3 tablespoons fresh lemon juice

Whipped cream and preserved cherries

1. **To make the babas,** combine the flour, yeast, sugar, and salt in the bowl of a stand mixer fitted with a dough hook. Add the eggs, ⅓ cup (80 ml) of the milk, and the melted butter. Knead on medium-high speed until the dough is soft and silky, about 8 minutes. Cover with a kitchen towel. Let rise until the dough doubles in volume, about 1½ hours. When you push down with your finger, the dough should feel firm and elastic.

2. Grease and flour 8 cups of a popover pan or large muffin pan. Divide the dough into 8 equal pieces (about 2½ ounces/70 g each) and form each into a ball; place them in the pan. Cover with a kitchen towel and let rise until noticeably puffy, about 30 minutes.

3. While the babas are rising, preheat the oven to 350°F (180°C).

4. Beat the egg yolk and the remaining 1 tablespoon milk together in a small bowl. Gently brush the babas with the egg wash. Bake until golden brown, 30 to 40 minutes.

5. While the babas are baking, make the syrup. Combine the cherry liqueur, sugar, and lemon juice with 2 cups (480 ml) water in a medium saucepan. Bring to a boil, stirring until the sugar dissolves. Remove from the heat and let cool slightly.

6. Remove the babas from the pan and place them in a large, shallow dish. Pour half the syrup over the warm babas. Allow them to soak up all of the liquid. Turn them over and repeat with all but about 3 tablespoons of the rest of the syrup. Transfer the babas to the fridge to chill for 1 to 2 hours.

7. Bring to room temperature before serving. Sprinkle the reserved syrup over the tops of the babas. Garnish with whipped cream and preserved cherries.

ORANGE-APPLE PIE
with Meringue and Streusel
Szarlotka

One day, I decided to give up sweets. (What a stupid idea!) I threw away all the chocolates I had saved for a rainy day and bought lots of chewing gum to neutralize my desire for cakes. I started counting down the days, to see how long I would last. Then I smelled a familiar scent—butter, cinnamon, and baked apples—my mom's apple cake. I just wanted to stare at it. The apple mousse was a beautiful gold, with a white, soft meringue hidden under a lavish amount of streusel. The crust looked so flaky and buttery, and I couldn't resist. I took a bite, and another, and another. Now I know that life without *szarlotka* doesn't make any sense.

MAKES	PREP TIME	COOK TIME	CHILLING TIME	BAKE TIME
8 servings	30 minutes	30 minutes	1 hour	55 minutes

FOR THE FILLING

1 tablespoon (15 g) unsalted butter

2 tablespoons grated orange zest (from 2 medium oranges)

3 pounds (1350 g) Golden Delicious apples, peeled, cored, cut into ¼- to ½-inch (8 mm) cubes

Juice of ½ lemon

½ cup (150 g) orange marmalade

1 tablespoon cornstarch

FOR THE DOUGH AND MERINGUE

3 cups (390 g) all-purpose flour

1 cup (200 g) sugar

1 teaspoon salt

20 tablespoons (2½ sticks/280 g) unsalted butter, chilled and cubed

3 large eggs, yolks and white separated

2 tablespoons cornstarch

1 vanilla bean, split lengthwise, or 1 teaspoon pure vanilla extract

3 tablespoons powdered sugar

recipe continues . . .

1. **To make the filling,** heat the butter in a large pot over medium heat. Add the orange zest and fry until fragrant, about 1 minute. Add the apples and lemon juice. Cook until the apples are soft and starting to break apart into applesauce. Add the orange marmalade and cornstarch; stir to combine. Let cool completely.

2. **To make the dough,** whisk together the all-purpose flour, ½ cup (100 g) of the sugar, and the salt. Add the butter, then use your fingers to rub it into the flour to make a light bread-crumb texture. Add the egg yolks and mix with a fork to combine.

3. Divide the dough into two parts in a ratio of about 70:30. Wrap the smaller part tightly in plastic wrap. Chill in the fridge for 1 hour, until firm.

4. While the smaller piece of dough is chilling, transfer the larger part of the dough to a 9-inch (23 cm) springform pan with a removable bottom. Using your fingertips, press the dough evenly onto the bottom and midway up the sides of the pan. Freeze until solid, about 15 minutes.

5. Preheat the oven to 375°F (190°C).

6. Prick the dough all over with a fork. Bake for about 15 minutes, until golden. Let cool completely, but leave the oven on.

7. **To make the meringue,** in the bowl of a stand mixer fitted with a whisk attachment, beat the egg whites on medium-high speed until white and foamy, about 1 minute. With the mixer running, gradually add the remaining ½ cup (100 g) sugar. Beat until firm peaks form, about 2 minutes longer. Scrape in the vanilla seeds (save the pod for another use). Add the cornstarch and stir to combine.

8. Spread the apple filling into the cooled crust. Gently spread the meringue over the filling, using a spatula. Grate the remaining dough and sprinkle it over the meringue. Bake for 35 to 40 minutes, until golden. Let cool, then cut into slices and serve with powdered sugar.

POPPY SEED ROLL

Makowiec

Every Christmas, Polish homes are filled with the scent of poppy seeds and buttery yeast dough baking in the oven. This delicacy is called *makowiec*, a roll lavishly filled with slivered almonds, crushed walnuts, honey, dried fruits, and, most importantly, poppy seeds, which are cooked in milk until soft. They're addicting. This recipe requires some patience for the dough, which should be kneaded, then allowed to rise, but trust me—the joy that comes from a still-warm slice far exceeds the labor involved in making it. For me, *makowiec* is a special cake that only appears one time of year, but I'm always willing to bake (and eat) it.

MAKES	PREP TIME	RISING TIME	BAKE TIME
2 rolls	30 minutes	2 hours	40 minutes

FOR THE DOUGH

2½ cups (320 g) all-purpose flour, plus more for shaping

¼ cup (50 g) sugar

One ¼-ounce (7 g) packet instant yeast

¼ teaspoon salt

3 large eggs

⅓ cup plus 1 tablespoon (95 ml) milk

½ cup (1 stick/115 g) unsalted butter, cubed

Vegetable oil

FOR THE FILLING

1 cup (140 g) poppy seeds

1 cup (240 ml) hot milk

½ cup plus 3 tablespoons (140 g) sugar

3 tablespoons honey

½ cup (40 g) slivered almonds

½ cup (50 g) walnuts, chopped

¼ cup (50 g) chopped dried apricots

2 tablespoons chopped candied orange zest

3 tablespoons orange liqueur

2 large eggs, yolks and whites separated

FOR THE ICING AND TOPPING

3 tablespoons fresh lemon juice

1 cup (130 g) powdered sugar

3 tablespoons chopped or slivered candied orange zest

recipe continues . . .

1. **To make the dough,** combine the flour, sugar, yeast, and salt in the bowl of a stand mixer fitted with a dough hook. Add 2 of the eggs and ⅓ cup (80 ml) of the milk. Knead on medium-high speed until fully combined; start adding the butter slowly, 1 tablespoon at the time. Knead until the dough is soft and silky, about 8 minutes.

2. Grease a large bowl and transfer dough to the bowl. Cover the bowl with a kitchen towel and let rise for 1½ hours, until tripled in size.

3. While the dough rises, make the filling. Grind the poppy seeds in a food processor until fluffy, then transfer to a large bowl. Pour in the hot milk. Let sit until the seeds absorb all the liquid, 20 to 30 minutes. Drain, if necessary.

4. Add ½ cup (100 g) of the sugar, the honey, almonds, walnuts, dried apricot, candied zest, orange liqueur, and egg yolks to the poppy seeds. In a separate medium bowl, beat the egg whites until peaks form, about 5 minutes. Continue beating, adding the remaining 3 tablespoons sugar, one at a time. Gently stir the whites into the poppy seed mixture.

5. Lightly flour a work surface and turn the dough out onto it. Sprinkle the dough with a little more flour and fold it over onto itself twice. Divide the dough into two equal parts. Roll out one part into an 8 x 4-inch (20 x 10 cm) rectangle on a lightly floured piece of parchment paper. Spread on half of the filling, keeping a 1-inch (2.5 cm) border all around. Using both hands, roll up the rectangle like a roulade, starting from the shorter side. Roll the dough completely into a perfect, thick log, sitting on its seam. Place the roll, still on the parchment paper, in a 9 x 5-inch (22 x 12 cm) loaf pan. Repeat with the remaining dough and filling. Cover both with kitchen towels and let rise until noticeable puffy, 30 to 40 minutes.

6. While the rolls are rising, preheat the oven to 350°F (180°C).

7. Beat the remaining egg and 1 tablespoon milk together in a small bowl. Gently brush the rolls with the egg wash. Bake until golden brown, 30 to 40 minutes. Cool in the pans for 15 minutes and then turn out onto a wire rack to cool completely.

8. **To make the icing,** heat the lemon juice in a small saucepan over low heat. Remove from the heat and stir in the powdered sugar, until well combined. Drizzle the glaze over the cooled rolls. Top with candied orange zest.

   Note: Makowiec will keep for up to 4 days at room temperature or can be frozen for up to 2 months, well-wrapped. It will dry out a bit, so I recommend reheating a slice in a pan with a bit of butter.

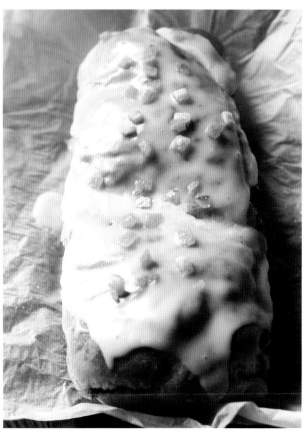

PRESERVES, JAMS, AND PICKLES

Konfitury, dżemy i kiszonki

I like the process of preparing preserves, jams, and pickles. It's like capturing summer in a jar, which you can open and taste at any time, even in the coldest days of December. I don't run a cannery in my apartment that makes several dozen jars every summer (though I know people who do), but I like to go to the market, pick the most beautiful fruits and vegetables, buy much more than I need, and make a lot of jams and preserves. It's always a worthy pursuit.

When it comes to jams and preserves, I like them to be special. I pair rose petals with raspberries in *Konfitura malinowa z płatkami różanymi* (Raspberry Preserves with Rose Petals, page 228), mix strawberries with lime and almonds in *Truskawkowo-limonkowa konfitura z płatkami migdałowymi* (Strawberry-Lime Preserves with Slivered Almonds, page 227), and combine apples with brown butter and cider in *Mus jabłkowy z cydrem i palonym masłem* (Brown Butter Applesauce with Cider, page 224). You can't easily get such things in a store. They also work beautifully as small gifts. I know, because after I give them away, my friends never stop talking about how delicious they are.

Pickles are a much more serious matter, but they're definitely worth it. Nothing tastes as good as *Ogórki kiszone* (Salt-Brined Dill Pickles, page 231), homemade fresh pickled cucumbers, which still have the freshness of raw cucumber, but with a slight fermented taste. I also recommend the *Kiszone rzodkiewki* (Salt-Brined Fermented Radishes, page 235), which are a great addition to salads.

PLUM JAM

Powidła śliwkowe

I love *powidła* because I am not a fan of super-sweet jams. *Powidła* is always made with plums, usually without additional sweeteners. Fine *powidła* requires a bit of careful cooking, but I think the work is worth it to achieve the necessary sweetness and consistency. The small amount of cinnamon and orange in this recipe make these plums even more delectable.

MAKES	PREP TIME	COOK TIME
two 12-ounce (350 ml) jars	10 minutes	2 hours

4½ pounds (2 kg) very ripe Italian or damson plums, halved and pitted

2 tablespoons (30 g) unsalted butter

1 teaspoon ground cinnamon

1 teaspoon grated orange zest

¼ cup (60 ml) orange juice

Up to 1 cup sugar (optional)

1. Place the plums, butter, cinnamon, orange zest, and juice in a large saucepan.

2. Cook for 1½ to 2 hours over low heat until almost all liquid evaporates. Stir frequently to keep the mixture from sticking to the bottom of the pan and burning. If your plums aren't very sweet or ripe, add sugar to taste.

3. While the jam cooks, wash the jars with soapy water, rinse well, and then heat in the oven at 250°F (120°C) for 15 minutes. Place the hot jam into the hot sterilized jars, leaving ¼ inch (7 mm) headspace. Cover with sterilized lids and rings. Bake at 350°F (180°C) for 10 minutes.

4. Allow the jam jars to cool completely on the counter before storing in a cool, dry, dark place.

   Note: Store in the pantry, unopened, for up to 1 year. If you don't bake the jars, the jam can be kept refrigerated for up to 3 weeks or frozen for up to 1 year.

BROWN BUTTER APPLESAUCE
with Cider
Mus jabłkowy z cydrem i palonym masłem

Poland is the country of the apple. We have so many varieties, but I like to pick crunchy and tart ones, such as Szara Reneta, which is perfect for *Szarlotka* (Orange-Apple Pie with Meringue and Streusel, page 211). Unfortunately, these types are not available in the US, but you can use other tart varieties, like Mutsu or Granny Smith instead. With nutty brown butter and hints of warm cardamom, this applesauce is abundant with fall apple flavor. Using dry apple cider keeps the sauce tart, which pairs perfectly with the creamy consistency.

	MAKES	COOK TIME
	2 cups	30 minutes

2 pounds (900 g) Mutsu or Granny Smith apples, peeled, cored, and chopped

¼ cup (50 g) sugar

1 tablespoon fresh lemon juice

½ cup (120 ml) dry apple cider

½ teaspoon ground cardamom

¼ cup (½ stick/60 g) unsalted butter

1. Combine the apples, sugar, lemon juice, cider, and cardamom in a medium saucepan. Bring to a boil; cook, uncovered, over low heat, stirring occasionally, until the apples are tender and falling apart, 20 to 30 minutes. Remove from the heat.

2. Meanwhile, make the brown butter. Heat the butter in a medium saucepan over low heat until it turns golden brown and starts smelling like nuts, 6 to 8 minutes. Remove from the heat.

3. Stir the brown butter into the applesauce. Pour the applesauce into jars. Store in the fridge up to 5 days.

STRAWBERRY-LIME PRESERVES
with Slivered Almonds

Truskawkowo-limonkowa konfitura z płatkami migdałowymi

One summer, my mother and I became obsessed with making preserves. We drove to the farmers market for the sweetest fruits. That's when we came up with the idea of strawberry preserves with slivered almonds, which add a pleasant crunch, and a lot of refreshing lime.

MAKES	PREP TIME	COOK TIME
three 12-ounce (350 ml) jars	10 minutes	20 minutes

2 pounds (900 g) strawberries, hulled and quartered

2 cups (400 g) sugar

1 tablespoon (15 g) unsalted butter

1 teaspoon powdered pectin

⅔ cup (60 g) slivered almonds

Juice and grated zest of 1 lime

1. Put the strawberries and sugar in a large saucepan. Cook, stirring occasionally, over low heat until juices are released, about 10 minutes.

2. Stir in the butter, pectin, almonds, and the lime juice and zest. Bring to a boil, and cook, stirring occasionally, for 10 minutes, until shiny.

3. While the jam cooks, wash the jars with soapy water, rinse well, and then heat the empty jars in the oven at 250°F (120°C) for 15 minutes. Place the hot jam into the hot sterilized jars, leaving ¼ inch (7 mm) headspace. Cover with sterilized lids and rings. Bake at 350°F (180°C) for 10 minutes.

4. Allow the jam jars to cool completely on the counter before storing in a cool, dry, dark place.

   Note: These preserves can be stored in the pantry, unopened, for up to 1 year.

   Multiply the recipe, if desired.

RASPBERRY PRESERVES
with Rose Petals

Konfitura malinowa z płatkami różanymi

This one is not very sweet, with the natural sourness of raspberry and sophisticated flavor of rose petals. It's a very elegant combination that will surely be remembered for a long time. It's one of my favorites to spread on morning challah.

MAKES	PREP TIME	COOK TIME
four 8-ounce (237 ml) jars	20 minutes	2 hours

3 pounds (1,350 g) raspberries

2 cups (400 g) sugar

Juice of 1 lemon

1 tablespoon (15 g) unsalted butter

3 tablespoons dried rose petals

2 tablespoons rose water

1. Toss the raspberries, sugar, and lemon juice in a large heavy pot. Let sit until the raspberries start to release their juices, about 20 minutes.

2. Bring the raspberry mixture to a boil, then add the butter. Cook over low heat, stirring occasionally at first and then more often as the mixture thickens (as the sugars concentrate, the preserves will be more likely to scorch), until most of the liquid evaporates and the preserves thicken, 2 hours. About 1½ hours into cooking, stir in the rose petals.

3. Remove from the heat and add the rose water.

4. While the jam cooks, wash the jars with soapy water, rinse well, and then heat the empty jars in the oven at 250°F (120°C) for 15 minutes. Place the hot preserves into the hot sterilized jars, leaving ¼ inch (7 mm) headspace. Cover with sterilized lids and rings. Bake at 350°F (180°C) for 10 minutes.

5. Allow the jam jars to cool completely on the counter before storing, unopened, in a cool, dry, dark place (or the refrigerator). Store for up to 5 months.

SALT-BRINED DILL PICKLES

Ogórki kiszone

Salt-brined pickles are prepared using the traditional process of natural fermentation in a brine that makes them grow sour. There's no vinegar or sugar here. The fermentation process is dependent on the *Lactobacillus* bacteria that naturally occur on the skin of growing cucumbers. These may be removed during commercial harvesting and packing processes, so it's best to choose cucumbers from a farmers market, if possible. Kirby cucumbers are perfect here.

MAKES	PREP TIME	FERMENTING TIME
one 3-quart (3 L) jar	15 minutes	5 days

4 tablespoons fine sea salt

2 quarts (2 L) mineral water

4 pounds (3.64 kg) Kirby cucumbers

1 head garlic

1 whole dill sprig with umbels and green seeds

One 1-inch (2.5 cm) piece horseradish root

4 unsprayed grape leaves

1 teaspoon mustard seeds

1. Wash a jar very carefully, then dry. In a large measuring cup or pitcher, dissolve the sea salt in the mineral water.

2. Put half of the cucumbers into the jar. Add the garlic, dill sprig, horseradish, grape leaves, and mustard seeds, then the rest of the cucumbers. Pour the brine over the cucumbers, leaving 1 to 2 inches (2.5 to 5 cm) headspace. Make sure that all cucumbers are covered with the brine (if not, remove one or two cucumbers from the jar). Cover the jar with a tight lid.

3. Ferment at room temperature for 24 hours. The brine should turn cloudy and bubbly. Transfer the jar to a refrigerator or any cold place (like a basement). After 4 days, you should have crunchy half-sour pickles. After 3 to 4 weeks, you should have softer full-sour pickles. Store in a dark, cool place for up to 6 months.

   Note: You can make these pickles in a few smaller jars, rather than in one big one.

   Don't worry about bubbles or a hissing sound—it means that the fermentation is working. But if you see any mold, or if the pickles are empty inside, discard them. The final product shouldn't be mushy.

SAUERKRAUT

Kiszoną kapustą

Preparing sauerkraut at home is not as popular as making dill pickles. The process is a bit more difficult and time-consuming, but it's worth it—especially when the result is really delicious.

MAKES	PREP TIME	FERMENTING TIME
one 3-quart (3 L) jar	15 minutes	5 days

4 tablespoons fine sea salt

2 quarts (2 L) mineral water

1 head green cabbage (2 pounds/900 g)

1 teaspoon salt

1 medium apple (7 ounces/200g), cored and sliced

4 bay leaves

1. Wash a jar very carefully, then dry. In a large measuring cup or pitcher, dissolve the sea salt in the mineral water.

2. Core and thinly slice the cabbage, then transfer to a large bowl and sprinkle with the salt. Knead the cabbage with clean hands until you see liquid (use the liquid in the brine).

3. Place the cabbage along with the sliced apple and bay leaves in the jar. Pour the salted mineral water over the cabbage, leaving 1 to 2 inches (2.5 to 5 cm) headspace (you don't want the liquid to touch the top of the lid, as it will end up overflowing). Make sure that the cabbage is fully covered (if not, remove some cabbage from the jar). Cover the jar with a tight lid.

4. Ferment at room temperature for about 2 weeks. The sauerkraut should be softened and nicely acidic. Store the jar in the refrigerator for up to a few months.

    Note: Don't worry about bubbles or a hissing sound—it means that the fermentation is working. But if you see any mold, discard the sauerkraut. The final product shouldn't be mushy.

SALT-BRINED FERMENTED RADISHES

Kiszone rzodkiewki

If I had to choose the most surprising fermented vegetable—in a positive way—it would be radishes. I'm not the only one who feels this way, because recently these little pink beauties have become very popular in trendy restaurants. Pickled radishes are soft but still crispy, ideal for a refreshing snack. They can also be used as a relish, like in the *Sałatka ziemniaczana z kiszonymi rzodkiewkami i gruszką* (Potato Salad with Fermented Radishes and Pear, page 128). What I like the most about this recipe is the touch of honey and allspice, which bring a whole new level of flavor to these vegetables.

MAKES	PREP TIME	FERMENTING TIME
one 3-quart (3 L) jar	15 minutes	5 days

4 tablespoons fine sea salt

2 tablespoons honey

2 quarts (2 L) mineral water

4 to 6 bunches radishes (1½ pounds/675 g total)

1 tablespoon allspice berries

1. Wash a jar very carefully, then dry. Dissolve the sea salt and honey in the mineral water.

2. Remove and discard the leaves and stalks from the radishes. Place the radishes and allspice into the jar. Pour the brine over the radishes, leaving 1 to 2 inches (2.5 to 5 cm) headspace (you don't want the liquid to touch the top of the lid, as it will end up overflowing). Make sure that all radishes are covered by the brine (if not, remove some radishes from the jar). Cover the jar with a tight lid.

3. Ferment at room temperature for 4 to 5 days. Store the jar in a refrigerator for up to a few months.

   Note: You can make four 1-pint (500 ml) jars instead of one large one.

   Don't worry about bubbles or a hissing sound—it means that the fermentation is working. But if you see any mold, discard the radishes. The final product shouldn't be mushy.

POPPED BUCKWHEAT

Popcorn z kaszy gryczanej

This recipe is an ode to buckwheat. The flavor is extremely nutty and smells divine. Popped buckwheat is not light like classic popcorn, but the crunchiness presents an opportunity to use it as a topping. I love to garnish my *Gołąbki z ziemniakami i kaszą* (Potato-Buckwheat *Gołąbki* with Tomato-Vodka Sauce, page 106) with it.

MAKES	COOK TIME
¾ cup	10 minutes

3 cups (720 ml) sunflower oil

½ cup (100 g) whole buckwheat (kasha)

Flaky sea salt

1. Heat the oil in a small saucepan over medium heat. Fry 1 to 2 tablespoons of the buckwheat kernels at a time, 5 to 10 seconds, until they begin to pop. Scoop the popped kernels out of the oil with a fine-mesh sieve and drain on a paper towel. Repeat until all the buckwheat has been cooked.

2. Sprinkle with sea salt. Serve as a snack or topping (for example, on pierogi), warm or at room temperature.

ACKNOWLEDGMENTS

Nearly everything in this book fills me with nostalgia. It makes me remember the friends and family members who inspired me to cook the dishes that appear on these pages. The biggest influences, of course, are my mother, Anna, and grandmother, Zosia. They taught me the joy of eating and inspired my need to feed others. Thank you for that. I love you.

So many of my friends helped me that I cannot thank them all—but I am so grateful for them. They have supported me all my life and helped me to become who I am now—a proud cook and food writer. They helped me during the most difficult times and always knew what to say to cheer me up when I needed it. I'm talking about you mostly: Zosia, Patrycja, Karolina, and Wiktoria. Thanks to all my friends who willingly eat the food I prepare—and always thank me for it. I appreciate you very much.

I would like to thank my friends who helped me to capture the beauty in this cookbook during the photo shoots. You were truly the best models and kitchen help: Wiktoria Aleksandrowicz, Katarzyna Pruszkiewicz, Krzysiek Marcinkowski, Wiktoria Szczepanowska, Wojtek Rożdżeński, and Zosia Zając. You can see the hands of these last three friends on the front cover.

I would also like to thank all the people who believed in me: the editors of *Saveur* magazine who chose to award me Best Food Blog Photographer when I was only nineteen; the editor-in-chief of the Polish magazine *Kuchnia,* Ewa Wagner, who gave me my first chance to write about food; and The Experiment, for proposing I write a cookbook and having an enthusiastic approach to my vision.

I thank my editors, Olivia Peluso and Jennifer Kurdyla, for their valuable advice and for seeing this book through every page; Beth Bugler, for designing it and making it beautiful; and everyone else at The Experiment, who helped make this cookbook truly special.

Judy Linden, thank you for being the best literary agent. Your support and help are indescribable.

I can't forget about the rest of my family. I'd especially like to thank my dad, for being so patient with my crazy food ideas, and my brother, for creating the website page for my blog. The journey started with this.

Last but not least, thank you to the readers of my Instagram and blog, Rozkoszny.pl, who cook with me every day and trusted me from the very beginning. This cookbook exists because of you.

INDEX

Page numbers in *italics* refer to photos.

ABOUT THE AUTHOR

MICHAŁ KORKOSZ won the 2017 *Saveur* Blog Award for best food photography (both Editors' and Readers' Choice). He is a food journalist, cake lover, and croissant gourmand. On his blog, Rozkoszny (which means "delightful"), he connects this love of cooking with another hobby—photography that captures both his delicious dishes and the loved ones he shares them with. He was born and raised in Poland.